INDEX OF AUTHORS, ETC.

Addison, 6.
Aeschylus, 5.
Africa, Stories of, 13.
Ainsworth (W. Harrison), 8.
À Kempis (Thomas), 13.
Aksakoff (Serghei), 4.
American Criticism, 4, 10.
American Verse, 4.
Ancient Law. 13.
Apocrypha The (R. V.), 13.
Aristophanes, 5.
Arnold (Matthew), 11.
Aurelius (Marcus), 11, 13.
Austen (Jane), 8.
Austrian Short Stories, 13.

Bacon (Francis), 11
Bagehot (Walter) 12.
Barrow (Sir John), 10.
Beaumont and Fletcher, 6.
Blackmore (R. D.), 8.
Blake (William), 11.
Borrow (George), 3, 14.
British Colonial Policy, 13.
   Foreign Policy, 13.
Brontë Sisters, 8 11.
Browning (Robert), 6, 11.
Buckle (T. H.), 10, 12
Buddha, Sayings of the, 13.
Bunyan (John), 8.
Burke, 12.
Burns (Robert), 11.
Butler, 8.
Byron (Lord), 11.

Carlyle (Thomas), 5, 6, 10.
Cellini (Benvenuto), 4.
Cervantes, 8.
Chaucer, 11.
Chesterfield, 10.
Cobbold (Richard), 8.
Coleridge (S. T.), 10, 11.
Collins (Wilkie), 8.
Colman, 6.
Confucius, 13.
Congreve (William), 6, 11.
Cooper (J. Fenimore), 8.
Cowper (William), 10.
Crabbe, 5.
Crime and Detection, 13.
Critical Essays, 3, 7, 10.
Czech Tales, 14.

Dante, 3, 11.
Darwin (Charles), 11.
Defoe (Daniel), 8.
Dekker, 6.
De Quincey (Thomas), 4.
Dickens (Charles), 8, 14.

Disraeli (Benjamin), 8.
Dobson (Austin), 5, 7, 11.
Don Quixote, 8.
Douglas (George), 8.
Dryden, 5, 6.
Dufferin (Lord), 10, 14.

Eighteenth-Century Comedies,
Eliot (George), 8.
Elizabethan Comedies, 6.
Elizabethan Tragedies, 6.
Emerson (R. W.), 7.
English Critical Essays, 7, 10.
English Essays, 3, 4.
English Prose, 4.
English Sermons, 7.
English Short Stories, 3, 4, 14.
English Songs and Ballads, 4, 11.
English Speeches, 12.
English Verse, 4, 11.

Farquhar, 6.
Fielding (Henry), 6, 8.
Four Gospels, 13.
Francis (St.), 5, 11.
Franklin (Benjamin), 4.
French Short Stories, 14.
Froude (J. A.), 7.

Galt (John), 8.
Gaskell (Mrs.), 5, 8, 14.
Gay, 6.
German Short Stories, 14.
Ghosts and Marvels, 14.
Gibbon (Edward), 4, 10.
Gil Blas, 9.
Goethe, 6, 11, 12.
Goldsmith (Oliver), 6, 8, 11.
Gray (Thomas), 10, 11.

Harris (J. C.), 8.
Harte (Bret), 14.
Hawthorne (Nathaniel), 8, 14.
Haydon (B. R.), 5.
Hazlitt (William), 5, 7, 10.
Herrick (Robert), 11.
Holme (Constance), 8, 14.
Holmes (Oliver Wendell), 7.
Homer, 5, 12.
Hood (Thomas), 12.
Horne (R. H.), 7.
Houghton (Lord), 5.
Hunt (Leigh), 5, 7.

Ibsen (Henrik), 6, 12.
Inchbald (Mrs.), 6.
Ingoldsby Legends, 11.
International Affairs, 13.
Irving (Washington), 7, 10, 14.

INDEX OF AUTHORS, ETC.

Johnson (Samuel), 5, 10.
Keats, 12.
Keble (John), 12.
Keith (A. B.), 13.
Kingsley (Henry), 9.
Koran, The, 13.
Lamb (Charles), 7.
La Motte Fouqué, 9.
Landor (W. S.), 7.
La Rochefoucauld, 7.
Lesage, 9.
Longfellow (H. W.), 12.
Macaulay (T. B.), 5, 10, 12.
Machiavelli, 12.
Mackenzie (Compton), 9.
Maine, Sir Henry, 13.
Marcus Aurelius, 11, 13.
Marlowe (Christopher), 6, 12.
Marryat (Captain), 9.
Massinger, 6.
Maude (Aylmer), 3, 5.
Meinhold (J. W.), 9.
Melville (Herman), 9, 14.
Mill (John Stuart), 5, 13.
Milton (John), 7, 12.
Montaigne, 7.
More (Paul Elmer), 10.
Morier (J. J.), 9, 14.
Morris (W.), 12.
Morton, 6.
Motley (J. L.), 10.
Murphy, 6.
Narrative Verse, 4, 12.
New Testament, 13.
Old Testament, 13.
Otway, 6.
Palgrave (F. T.), 4.
Pamphlets and Tracts, 4, 7.
Peacock (T. L.), 9.
Peacock (W.), 4.
Persian (From the), 14.
Poe (Edgar Allan), 14.
Polish Tales, 14.
Prescott (W. H.), 10.
Pre-Shakespearean Comedies, 6.
Rabelais, 3, 9.
Reading at Random, 4.
Redman (B. R.), 4.
Restoration Tragedies, 6.
Reynolds (Frederick), 6.

Reynolds (Sir Joshua), 7.
Rossetti (Christina), 12.
Rowe, 6.
Ruskin (John), 7, 13.
Russian Short Stories, 14.
Rutherford (Mark), 7.
Sainte-Beuve, 10.
Scott (Sir W.), 5, 9, 12, 14.
Scottish Verse, 4, 12.
Sermons (English), 7, 13.
Shakespeare, 6, 12.
Shakespeare Criticism, 10.
Shakespeare's Predecessors and Contemporaries, 6.
Shelley, 12.
Sheridan (R. B.), 6.
Smith (Adam), 13.
Smith (Alexander), 7.
Smollett (T.), 7, 9, 14.
Sophocles, 5.
Southerne, 6.
Southey (Robert), 10.
Spanish Short Stories, 14.
Stanhope (Lord), 5.
Steele, 6.
Sterne (Laurence), 7, 9, 14.
Stevenson (R. L.), 7, 9.
Sturgis, 9.
Swift (Jonathan), 9.
Swinburne, 12.
Swinnerton (Frank), 9.
Taylor (Meadows), 9.
Tennyson (Lord), 12.
Thackeray (W. M.), 9.
Three Dervishes, The, 14.
Tolstoy, 3, 5, 6, 7, 9, 11, 13, 14.
Tracts and Pamphlets, 4, 7.
Trevelyan, 5.
Trollope (Anthony), 3, 5, 9, 14.
Virgil, 5, 12.
Walpole (Hugh), 9.
Walton (Izaak), 5, 8.
Watts-Dunton (Theodore), 9.
Webster, 6.
Wellington (Duke of), 5.
Wells (Charles), 12.
Wells (H. G.), 4.
Wharton (Edith), 9.
White (Gilbert), 8, 10.
Whitman (Walt), 8, 12.
Whittier (J. G.), 12.
Wordsworth (William), 12.

Further Volumes are in preparation.

January 1940

PRINTED IN GREAT BRITAIN

198 An example of skid conditions occurring in summer is when a shower of rain follows a long dry spell. This results in the road surface becoming a gooey mixture of rubber shreds, oil splashes and water, which could be absolutely lethal to a driver who is unaware of the changed conditions.

199 Dangerous times (as opposed to conditions) are:
    a Rush hours.
    b Public Houses closing times.
    c Times at which schoolchildren are on their way to and from school.
    d Scheduled times for major sporting events.

200 Aquaplaning is the effect which results from driving too fast on a very wet surface. It occurs when tyres in less than perfect condition begin to lose their direct grip on the road surface and ride on the surface of the water in the same manner as water skis. The condition may be recognised by a loss of steering response. In such a case, reduce speed by deceleration and on no account touch the brakes or a complex skid will result.

    A very approximate estimation of the speed at which aquaplaning may occur is to multiply the square root of your tyre pressure by nine.

    Example: Tyre pressure 25 lb per sq inch — the square root of 25 is 5 — hence $5 \times 9 = 45$. Therefore aquaplaning could be expected to commence at around 45 mph.

At the time of going to press, legislation is going through Parliament which may affect Answers 3 and 67. Readers are therefore advised to watch for press announcements regarding these.

Notes

New words

authorities
people who rule

brain
the mind; grey matter inside the head that we use when we think

disgusting
very nasty, making one feel sick

experiment
a scientist's work, finding the result of doing certain things

flash
a sudden bright light

French
of France

glacier
a slow-moving river of ice

horror
a feeling of great fear

human
of men, women and children

kite
paper or cloth over a very light arrangement of wood; we make it fly on the end of a long string

lightning
a flash of electricity in the sky in a storm

monster
a very large, strange and frightening animal or person

publish
print and sell books: a **publisher** arranges for books to be printed and sold

thunder
the sound of an electric storm

university
a place of learning that one goes to after leaving school

Questions on the whole story

These are harder questions. Read the Introduction, and think hard about the questions before you answer them. Some of them ask for your opinion, and there is no fixed answer.

1 Thackeray called *Vanity Fair* "a novel without a hero". Here are lists of some of the main people in the story. Can you give ONE reason, and an example, in each case for *not* calling the person a "hero" or a "heroine"? (Example: *Jos Sedley* was not brave. For example, he ran away from Brussels, leaving Amelia.)
Heroes? a Lieutenant George Osborne;
b Rawdon Crawley; c Dobbin
Heroines? d Amelia Sedley; e Rebecca Sharp; f Miss Crawley

2 Now name ONE good point in each of the people named in Question 1, and give an example. (Example: *Jos Sedley* tried to be a good son. For example, he sent money to his parents when they needed it.)

3 What, in your opinion, was *a* the worst, and *b* the best thing that Becky did?

4 What is amusing or funny in these examples of Thackeray's writing?
 a "There was another reason for Rawdon and Becky to leave London and take the best rooms at the best hotel in Brighton. They had no money." (page 28)
 b "One day, Dobbin arrived in a carriage, bringing a wooden horse, a drum, and other warlike toys for little Georgy – who was hardly six months old." (page 45)
 c "The new Governor of Coventry Island didn't die of yellow fever until he had been four years on the island." (page 61)

5 "It is true that the Raggles's happy life was entirely destroyed by the Crawleys' use of his house, Raggles himself being sent to prison for debt. But *somebody* has to pay, even for gentlemen who live on nothing a year." – What, in your opinion, did Thackeray really think about such "gentlemen"?

New words

awkward
not moving or acting easily; appearing to do things with difficulty

billiards
a game played on a cloth-covered table with pockets into which the balls are hit

butler
head manservant

cavalry
soldiers who fought on horseback

coach
a large carriage pulled by four horses, taking passengers inside and on top

companion
a woman who (like Miss Briggs) was paid to help and be the friend of another

conscience
an inner sense that tells us when an action is wrong

debt
money that is owed; in debt = owing money to another person or other people

defeat
beat; being beaten in war

duel
a fight (with pistols, hand guns) to settle a quarrel

fashion
rich people's way of dressing or behaving at a particular time; **fashionable** = in the latest fashion

governess
a woman who lives in the home and educates the children of the family

imitate
copy another person's way of behaving, speaking, etc

income
the amount of money which a person receives every year

innocent
not having done anything wrong

regiment
a large group of soliders (1,000 or more) under the command of a **colonel**

staff
the officers who help a general in his work of commanding a number of **regiments**

Index

A
Ageing 6, 8, 17, 36, 59-74
  anti-ageing and antioxidant nutrients 59-74
Alcohol 17-18, 43, 52-4
  red wine 52-4
Alzheimer's Disease 61, 64-6
Antioxidant compounds see Flavonoids
Antioxidant minerals see Minerals, antioxidant
Antioxidant vitamins see Vitamins, antioxidant
Arthritis 8, 36, 42, 67-9

B
Bacteria 9, 50, 53
Beta-carotene 6-7, 11, 14-15, 24-31, 56, 62-4, 68-71, 73-5
  and anti-ageing 62-4, 68-71
  and cancer 27-8
  and cataracts 64
  definition of 25-7
  and skin care 26, 69-71
Blood 7, 9, 13, 36, 41-2, 57-8, 62, 66
  haemoglobin, production of 41-2

C
Cancer 6, 8, 14, 16-17, 21, 27-9, 33, 39, 44-6, 50-6, 58
  and beta-carotene 27-8
  and flavonoids 51-6, 58
  of the skin 16-17
  and selenium 44-6
  and vitamin C 33
  see also Smoking
Carotenoids 6-7, 11, 14-15, 24-31, 56, 62-4, 68-71, 73-5
  Beta-carotene 6-7, 11, 14-15, 24-31, 56, 62-4, 68-71, 73-5
  carotenoid composition of foods 29-30
Cataracts 6, 8, 63-4
Copper 6, 40-2, 77

D
DNA (deoxyribonucleic acid) 10-11, 75-6
Drugs, prescription 7

E
Enzymes 8-9, 11, 13, 40-1, 43, 50-1, 60, 71-2, 75, 77
  antioxidant enzyme SOD 40, 77
Eyes 6, 8, 44, 63-4

F
Fats/lipids 11, 18-20, 55, 76
  cooking oils 18-20
  lipid peroxidation 11
  lipoproteins 76
Flavonoids 18, 32-3, 50-8, 66, 71-2
  Bioflavonoids 32-3
  and cancer 51-6, 58
  and heart disease 50, 52-6, 58
  herbal remedies 57-8, 66
Free radicals 7-23, 26, 59-62, 65-6, 68-9, 71-2, 75-6
  and ageing 59-62, 65-6, 68-9, 71-2
  avoidance of pollutants 12-23
  definition of 9, 75-6
  and DNA 10-11
  increased exposure to 9-10
Fruit 6, 22, 25-30, 32, 34-5, 37, 50, 54-5, 60, 73

G
Genetics 21

H
Heart disease 6, 8, 20, 33, 35-8, 44-7, 50, 52-6, 58, 73, 75
  and flavonoids 50, 52-6, 58

79

ANTIOXIDANTS

and selenium 46-7
and vitamin E 37-8, 55
Herbs/herbal remedies 6, 57-8, 66

I
Immune system 6, 9, 13, 35, 43-4, 62-3, 67

L
Lung disease 8, 13-14, 27-8, 31, 33, 54-6

M
Manganese 6, 40-1, 54, 77
Minerals, antioxidant 6, 13, 40-9, 54, 63, 77
 and see specifically
  Copper,
  Manganese,
  Selenium, Zinc

O
Oxidation 7-8, 11, 24, 52, 55, 62, 70, 76
Ozone 8, 13, 17, 76
 ozone layer 17

P
Parkinson's disease 8, 66-7
Peroxidation 18-19
Pollution/pollutants 10, 12-15, 43, 45, 69, 71, 76

Polyphenols
 see Flavonoids

R
Radiation 15-17, 26, 69-72

S
Selenium 6, 40, 44-9
 and cancer 44-6
 and heart disease 46-7
Skin 15-17, 31-2, 36, 41, 43-4, 61, 69-74
 ageing/wrinkling 61, 69-74
 skincare products 36, 69-72
Smoking 12, 14-15, 43, 45, 71, 76
Supplements, mineral/ vitamin 7, 22, 48, 63, 72-4

T
Tea, properties of 52-4, 56

V
Vegetables 6, 22, 25-30, 32, 34-5, 37, 42-3, 50, 54-5, 60, 73
Vitamins, antioxidant 6-11, 13-15, 18-19, 22-39, 42, 45, 50, 52, 55-7, 59-75
 and action 6-11
 and anti-ageing 59-74

 see specifically
  Beta-carotene,
  Vitamin C,
  Vitamin E
Vitamin A
 see Beta-carotene, Carotenoids
Vitamin C 6-7, 11, 14-15, 18, 22-4, 30-5, 42, 45, 50, 55-7, 63-4, 67-72, 75
 and anti-ageing 63-4, 67-71
 and cancer 33
 and cataracts 64
 cooking tips 34-5
 and skin care 69-71
Vitamin E 6-7, 11, 13-15, 19, 22-4, 35-9, 45, 52, 55-6, 62-4, 67-75
 and anti-ageing 62-4, 67-72
 and cataracts 64
 cooking tips 38-9
 and heart disease 37-8, 55
 and skin care 69-72

W
Water, drinking 20-1

Z
Zinc 6, 40, 42-4, 77

Svar:

1. ....
2. ....
3. ....
4. ....
5. ....
6. ....
7. ....
8. ....
9. ....
10. ....
11. ....
12. ....
13. ....
14. ....
15. ....
16. ....
17. ....
18. ....
19. ....
20. ....
21. ....
22. ....
23. ....
24. ....
25. ....
26. ....
27. ....
28. ....
29. ....
30. ....

The chariot rumbled nearer. She stood her ground. The great bronze hands of the clock jerked round and the bell began to toll.

The flowers of spring smelt sweet.

Almost on her . . .

She flew up, a white dove, and perched on the chariot.

The Demon King cried out in rage, staring about, seeking her. Perched behind him she ruffled her feathers, shrank in on herself.

Long, sinuous, heavy as clay, implacable, the python wound around the Demon King and sighed his breath away.

The demon's bones cracked. The snake loosened its coils and dropped the body into the dust.

Taking the reins Sam turned the chariot. She felt a warmth around her neck where hung the Elixir of Life. Slowly she drove into the waiting city.

Next evening when she came home from school there was a holly wreath on the front door.

'That's nice,' she said, surprised.

'Mm, I thought we should do something a bit festive,' said Sara. She seemed to be in a good mood, and the hall was full of decorations.

And at dinnertime she produced three glasses and a bottle of champagne.

'What's this in aid of?' asked Mike, startled but willing.

'I've got a job,' said Sara. 'I'm going to work with Rachel at the Women's Centre.'

The cork exploded from the bottle and bounced round the room. Tai caught it as it rolled past her and dribbled it under the table. Sara poured the champagne.

'Well done,' said Mike.

'That's great, Mum,' said Sam.

They clinked their glasses together.

On Saturday afternoon it was the Club Christmas party. It was held then so that the prisoners could attend. They had a table to themselves on the other side of the room. Pete waved but he was busy talking to his mates.

Lucy was in an electric wheelchair with controls on the armrest. 'It came back from being mended last night,' she said. 'Just in time! Come and dance.'

'No, it's stupid,' said Sam.

'Please?'

Sam couldn't resist. She followed Lucy on to the floor feeling at first very embarrassed. But Lucy's face was alight with laughter as she spun her chair this way and that and suddenly Sam started to enjoy herself.

'Can I join in?' It was Pete, in a borrowed wheelchair. Round and round they went, twisting and turning, till the room was spinning and they were dizzy with laughter.

'That was good,' said Pete. 'Want a drink?'

Sam nodded, out of breath.

The girls went back to their table while Pete fetched some Coke.

'Let's pull a cracker,' said Sam.

Lucy held out her hand and Sam put one end of the cracker into it.

'I'm going to Africa,' said Lucy. 'I've decided, I'm going on safari. I'm going to be the world expert on elephants!'

'Great,' said Sam.

Bang went the cracker and out fell the usual assortment of a paper hat, a bad joke, and a lucky charm.

you boys decide to run away again, take me with you."

In the days that followed, ballad sellers began to cry out new and final verses to the notorious life of Hold-Your-Nose Billy and his partner, Cutwater.

An old rat-catcher had seen them flee from the sewer. And he'd seen them stow away aboard a ship raising its sails for a long voyage. It was a convict ship bound for a speck of an island in distant waters. A convict island.

Note

Readers often write to ask if a story is true. This tale is a work of the imagination, but the most surprising part of it is true.

Some royal households of past centuries did keep whipping boys to suffer the punishments due a misbehaving prince. History is alive with lunacies and injustices.

As Jemmy would say, "Gaw!"

TABLE

    I. Le monde de l'homme 9
   II. Les hommes sont le monde 13
  III. L'autre lumière 19
  IV. Le soleil et le feu 27
    V. La langue du monde 29
  VI. Les yeux de l'homme 31
 VII. Les sens des yeux 37
VIII. Les yeux animaux 39
  IX. Le chien rouge 53
    X. Le Kangourou 59
  XI. Le mouvement de la terre 63
 XII. Les limites de la terre 65
XIII. Les enfants, les femmes, les hommes 69
XIV. Le seul lieu où nous sommes 89

ACHEVÉ D'IMPRIMER
2ᵉ TRIMESTRE 1991
SUR LES PRESSES DE
L'IMPRIMERIE SZIKRA
90200 GIROMAGNY

ISBN : 2-7291-0699-5

INDEX DES THÈMES ET NOTIONS

(Les chiffres renvoient aux pages du Profil)

Amour, 41, 48, 49, 58, 63-66, 74, 76,

Angoisse, 27, 51, 58, 66,

Art, 24, 26, 43, 83,

Christ, 28, 30, 59, 71-73,

Conscience, 22, 27, 32, 48, 57, 70, 72, 78-79,

Corps, 57-58, 72,

Deuil, 65, 74,

Dignité, 30-33, 67,

Écoute, 40, 41, 55, 74-76,

Épopée, 90-91,

Érotisme, 37, 49,

Expressionnisme, 83, 85,

Femme, 42, 47-49, 63-66, 74-76,

Focalisation, 77-81,

Fraternité, 34, 58-59, 60, 70-76,

Groupe, 28, 54-62, 72,

Hasard, 25, 31, 44, 51,

Humiliation, humilié, 37, 45, 47, 49, 66-68,

Individu, 54-62,

Mal, 25, 29, 89,

Mémoire, souvenirs, 33, 41, 52-53, 66-68,

Misère, 31, 37-38, 45,

Mort, 24, 29, 30, 32-33, 39, 41, 44, 46, 52, 54, 65, 66, 69, 71-73, 76, 89, 90,

Prostitution, 42, 47-48,

Révolution, 28, 29, 30, 34, 35, 40, 48, 54, 61-62, 67, 86, 87, 89,

Sagesse, 39-42, 43-46,

Séparation, 57, 63-69,

Solitude, 30, 41, 54, 55-57, 65-66, 69,

Souffrance, 25, 31, 32, 34, 41, 58, 64-68,

Suicide, 24, 28, 30, 47, 48, 69,

Temps, 26, 31, 50-53

Terrorisme, 24, 29, 30, 55, 61-62, 83,

Théâtralité, 42-44,

Tragédie, tragique, 26, 51, 91-93,

Volonté, 54-55, 67, 89.

Achevé d'imprimer en France par la Nouvelle Imprimerie Laballery
Dépôt légal : 74078-7/07 – Février 2018 – N° d'impression : 802026

Fragrant Tea Blend

An instant but well-appreciated gift for a tea-loving friend.

2 parts Earl Grey tea
2 parts Lapsang Souchong tea
1 part Darjeeling tea

Mix together and put into a pretty, airtight container.

The Author

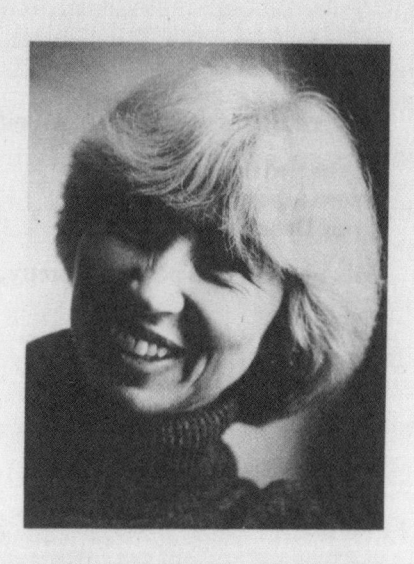

Patricia Lousada was born in New York City. Her Italian mother was a singer and an inspired cook with a wide knowledge of Italian and French cuisine. Patricia was a member of the New York City Ballet and her fellow dancers' love of good food further involved her in cooking. She later lived in Paris for two years, where the experience of attending lectures at the Cordon Bleu school, against a background of Parisian restaurants, deepened her interest still more. She has given lectures and demonstrations on various kinds of cooking.

Patricia has for a long time found that her cooking skills enable her to give friends and relatives delicious and unique presents, and she decided to share her many ideas in this book. Her previous two books for Sainsbury's were *Pasta Italian Style* and *American Sampler*.

Lady Lousada lives in London with her English husband and has four children.

Y Y Y Y Y

YIN or YANG

Yin and *yang* are Chinese terms describing the complementary (but opposed) principles which underlie religion, medicine and so on. The two go together like a horse and carriage – but which is which?

Yang is the 'active male principle', light and warm, while *yin* is the colder and more passive 'feminine principle', each necessary to the other, held in a state of balance and tension, etc. As with various imports from Chinese culture, such as *feng shui*, originally serious ideas have been largely reduced to advertising props or lifestyle adornments for the west:

> How clever of [hotel] owner Anouska Hempel to reflect 'the bi-polarity of the world between yin and yang, black and white, hot and cold...'
> (Daily Telegraph)

Embarrassment rating: ●○○ If you can't sort out your yins from your yangs, don't worry – unless you are in seriously New Agey circles. A little face might be saved by ensuring you pronounce *feng shui* correctly (say 'fung shway').

How to avoid: *Yin* contains -i-, as does fem*i*nine: *yang* contains -a-, as does m*a*sculine.

Z Z Z Z Z

ZENITH or NADIR

This is a which-way-round-is-it? difference which, I must confess, is included here partly for the satisfaction of having an entry under 'z'.

The *zenith* is the 'position in the sky directly over the observer's head', and so comes to mean 'high point', 'most flourishing period':

Evans grew up at the zenith of the Welsh coal industry, when one in four men worked in mining. (Guardian)

The *nadir* is the 'direct opposite of the zenith', and if taken literally would apply to the position under the observer's feet, but it is rarely used in this celestial or astronomical sense and means rather the 'lowest point', the 'worst period':

The 2002 A-level marking scandal was the nadir, a shambles of control-freakery, pseudo-privatisation and muddle. (The Times)

Embarrassment rating: ●●◐, since the words convey precisely opposite meanings.

How to avoid: The *zenith* is the high position overhead, the *nadir* is the point under the observer.

General bibliography

Cerney J.V., *ACUPRESSURE—Acupuncture without needles*, 1st edition, Simon & Schuster, 1974.

Ewart Charles, *THE HEALING NEEDLES*, 1st edition, Elm Tree Books, 1982.

Jayasuria Anton & Fernando Felix, *PRINCIPLES & PRACTICE OF SCIENTIFIC ACUPUNCTURE*, 1st edition, Jayasuria & Fernando, 1978.

Jayasuria Anton & Wijesinghe Lasath, *ANCILLIARY METHODS OF ACUPUNCTURE*, 1st edition, The Acupuncture Foundation of Sri Lanka, 1981.

Leger J.P., *THE LITTLE RED BOOK OF ACUPUNCTURE*, 1st edition, Thornsons, 1978.

Mann Felix, *ACUPUNCTURE, THE ANCIENT CHINESE ART OF HEALING AND HOW IT WORKS SCIENTIFICALLY*, 1st edition, Vintage Books, February, 1973.

Mary Austin, *ACUPUNCTURE THERAPY—Philosophy, Principles and Methods of Chinese Acupuncture*, ASI PUBLISHERS INC., 1972 1981.

Patel J.K. & Colleagues, *CLINICAL ACUPUNCTURE*, 1981, Indian Medical Acupuncture Training & Research Centre, Baroda.

Stiefwater Eric H.W. & Leslie O. Korth, *What is Acupuncture? How does it work?* 2nd edition, Health Science Press, 1971.

The Academy of Traditional Chinese Medicine, *AN OUTLINE OF CHINESE ACUPUNCTURE*, Foreign Language Press, Peking, 1975.

and content yourself; and trouble me not! (*He walks swiftly to the stairs. Then stops, realising that* CRANMER, *carrying his Bible, has followed him. Quite kindly.*) I beseech Your Grace, go back.

Offended, CRANMER *does so. The lighting is now complete, i.e., darkness save for three areas of light, the one at head of stairs now dazzlingly brilliant. When* MORE *gets to head of stairs by the* HEADSMAN *there is a single shout from the crowd. He turns to* HEADSMAN.

Friend, be not afraid of your office. You send me to God.
CRANMER (*envious rather than waspish*): You're very sure of that, Sir Thomas.
MORE (*takes off his hat, revealing the grey disordered hair*): He will not refuse one who is so blithe to go to him. (*Kneeling.*)

Immediately, harsh roar of kettledrums and total blackout at head of stairs. While the drums roar, WOMAN *backs into* CRANMER *and exit together.* NORFOLK *assists* MARGARET *from the stage, which is now 'occupied' only by the two spots left and right front. The drums cease.*
HEADSMAN (*from the darkness*): Behold – the head – of a traitor!

Enter into spots left and right, CROMWELL *and* CHAPUYS. *They stop on seeing one another, arrested in postures of frozen hostility while the light spreads plainly over the stage, which is empty save for themselves.*

Then simultaneously they stalk forward, crossing mid-stage with heads high and averted. But as they approach their exits they pause, hesitate, and slowly turn. Thoughtfully they stroll back towards one another. CROMWELL *raises his head and essays a smile.* CHAPUYS *responds. They link arms and approach the stairs. As they go we hear that they are chuckling. There is nothing sinister or malignant in the sound; rather it is the self-mocking, self-indulgent, rather rueful laughter of men who know what the world is and how to be comfortable in it. As they go,* THE CURTAIN FALLS.

ALTERNATIVE ENDING

In the London production of this play at the Globe Theatre the play ended as follows:

Instead of the CROMWELL *and* CHAPUYS *entrance after the* HEADSMAN'S *line* 'Behold – the head – of a traitor!', *the* COMMON MAN *came to the centre stage, having taken off his mask as the executioner, and said:*

'I'm breathing. . . . Are you breathing too? . . . It's nice isn't it? It isn't difficult to keep alive friends . . . just don't make trouble – or if you must make trouble, make the sort of trouble that's expected. Well, I don't need to tell you that. Good night. If we should bump into one another, recognise me.'

(*Exits*)

CURTAIN

The Marx Brothers
Monkey Business, Duck Soup, A Day at the Races
£8.99 FPB

Dudley Nichols
Stagecoach
£4.95 FPB

Harold Pinter
The Comfort of Strangers and Other Screenplays
£7.99 FPB
The French Lieutenant's Woman and Other Screenplays
£8.99 FPB
The Heat of the Day
£4.99 FPB
The Proust Screenplay
£9.99 FPB
The Servant and Other Screenplays
£8.99 FPB
The Trial
£8.99 FPB

Roman Polanski
Knife in the Water with *Repulsion* and *Cul-de-Sac*
£6.95 FPB

Dennis Potter
Lipstick on Your Collar
£8.99 FPB
The Singing Detective
£6.99 FPB

Sally Potter
Orlando
£6.99 FPB

Paul Schrader
Light Sleeper
£6.99 FPB

Taxi Driver
£5.99 FPB

Budd Schulberg
On the Waterfront
£7.99 FPB

Martin Scorsese and Nicholas Pileggi
GoodFellas
£5.99 FPB

Steven Soderbergh
sex, lies and videotape
£6.99 FPB

Whit Stillman
Barcelona and *Metropolitan*
£8.99 FPB

Tom Stoppard
Rozencrantz and Guildenstern are Dead: The Film
£5.99 FPB

Quentin Tarantino
Pulp Fiction
£8.99 FPB

Andrei Tarkovsky
Andrei Rublev
£9.99 FPB

Francois Truffaut
Jules et Jim
£4.99 FPB

Gus Van Sant
Even Cowgirls Get the Blues/My Own Private Idaho
£8.99 FPB

Robert Wiene
The Cabinet of Doctor Caligari
£4.99 FPB

MUSIC AND DIALOGUE FROM THE MOTION PICTURES

PULP FICTION
CD Cat no: MCD 11103
Cass. Cat no: MCC 11103

1. Dick Dale & His Del Tones *Misirlou*
2. Kool & The Gang *Jungle Boogie* 3. Al Green *Let's Stay Together* 4. The Tornadoes *Bustin' Surfboards*
5. Ricky Nelson *Lonesome Town* 6. Dusty Springfield *Son Of A Preacher Man* 7. The Centurians *Bullwinkle Part II* 8. Chuck Berry *You Never Can Tell* 9. Urge Overkill *Girl, You'll Be A Woman Soon* 10. Maria McKee *If Love Is A Red Dress (Hang Me In Rags)* 11. The Revels *Comanche* 12. The Statler Brothers *Flowers On The Wall* 13. The Lively Ones *Surf Rider*

MCA

RESERVOIR DOGS
CD Cat no: MCD 10793
Cass. Cat no: MCC 10793

1. The George Baker Selection *Little Green Bag*
2. Blue Swede *Hooked On A Feeling*
3. Joe Tex *I Gotcha* 4. Bedlam *Magic Carpet Ride*
5. Sandy Rogers *Fool For Love*
6. Stealers Wheel *Stuck In The Middle With You*
7. Bedlam *Harvest Moon* 8. Harry Nilsson *Coconut*

MCA

AVAILABLE FROM ALL GOOD RECORD SHOPS
or
VIA MAIL ORDER FROM
Dept F SELECT SOUNDTRACKS,
18 DALBY ROAD, LONDON SW18 1AW.

Enclose:- 1. Your name and your address.
2. Your crossed cheque, or postal order for £13.49 (CD) or £10.49 (cassette) made payable to SELECT SOUNDTRACKS.

FOR A CATALOGUE OF SOUNDTRACKS <u>ONLY</u> SEND
2 x 1st CLASS STAMPS TO THE ABOVE ADDRESS.

Personal statement by Richard Gere
and Cindy Crawford.................. 24
Pink Panther series, The............. 11
Planets visited 53
Police Academy gang, The............ 23
Porn actresses in mainstream movies..... 18
Potential tabloid headline movie titles 44
Prime directives of Robocop, The 30
Production company logos............. 48

R
Renoir, Jean....................... 69
Renowned prosthetic designers.......... 95
Republic serials 56
Resnais, Alain 91
Rules of Super Size Me, The 28
Running times of Director's Cuts........ 12
Rocky Balboa fight card............... 54
Rohmer, Eric, franchises............... 66

S
Sarris', Andrew, director categories 87
Schindler's List.....................100
Screen snogs....................... 80
Self Preservation Society, The 25
Shawshank Redemption, The poster girls of.. 80
Six stars who have been sued
for palimony...................... 32
6,469,952 70
Skipping rhyme (A Nightmare
On Elm Street), The.................. 6
Spanish short film with man trapped
in phone box 18
Spectacularly wrong reviews............ 57
Spencer, Bud and Hill, Terence 61
Spinal Tap, This Is 43
Sportsfolk-turned-actors 63
Split-screen sequences 13
Star Wars call signs 32
Stars and their phobias 32
Stars who have cameoed
in remakes of their hits 7
Stars who use their middle names
as first names.................... 68
Stephen King's alter egos 16
Stephen King novels not yet filmed 47
Stories remade 47
Suggested rentals for estate agents 73

T
Talents who never won an Oscar 86
Tarzans 7
Taxonomy of T-shirts worn in Teen Wolf.. 43

Taylor, Elizabeth, marriage soundbites.... 97
Ten directors who made adverts after
they got famous 90
Ten most horrific cinema fires, The 62
Ten movie DJs 78
Ten persistent rumours............... 35
Ten stars who died mid-shoot 83
Ten stars who have stayed at
The Betty Ford Clinic................ 27
They would have gotten away with
it if it weren't for.................... 22
Three Hats For Lisa.................. 19
THX-1138 references 55
Time Bandits 96
Titles that were just asking for it 45
Top ten years for cinema admissions, The.. 50
Top 20 US opening weekends, The....... 52
Top 20 highest grossing R-rated
movies, The 70
Tracy's face....................... 42

V
"Versus" movies (selected) 102
Vigo, Jean 8
Vintage number one hits that share titles
with movies 33

W
Warriors, The major gangs in........... 1
Wavelength....................... 54
Wet Nellie 37
Where you've seen the stars of The West
Wing before 21
What's the film about the plane that has
crash-landed in the desert?........... 21
What's the film where Paul Henreid lights
two cigarettes...?................... 8
What's the '70s film in which a truck chases
a car (not Duel)? 20
Which Carry On film are you watching? .. 36
Who is that?...................... 89
Whose voice is that?................. 17
Wilhelm Scream, The................. 67
Woody Allen's Manhattan 51
World's First Cinemas, The 85

Y
Yabba dabba...................... 53
Yuppie nostalgia 95

Z
Zero gravity toilet................... 31

EMPIRE MOVIE MISCELLANY

BIZARRE END CREDITS

The following is a list of curious, witty and downright weird job titles that have adorned the end credits of movies...

Spiritual Advisor (Patti Rocks)
Vomit Creature (Poltergeist II)
Massage Therapist (Ruby)
Additional Dialogue by William Shakespeare
(My Own Private Idaho)
Scooby-Doo Philosopher (Slacker)
Electrical Best Person As Opposed To Best Boy
(Slam Dance)
Naughty Best Boy
(The Adventures Of Priscilla, Queen Of The Desert)
Golf Advisor (The Two Jakes)
Catering... Kaos
(Highly recommended by the whole cast and crew)
(The Coca-Cola Kid)
Snow Management (A Midnight Clear)
Cheese Host (Made In Heaven)
Orgy Advisor (Solomon And Sheba)
Blob Wrangler (The Blob)
Sparrow Wrangler (The Dark Half)
Skunk Wrangler (Patti Rocks)
Roach Wrangler (Creepshow)
Sperm Wrangler (Look Who's Talking Too)
Ant Consultant (Empire Of The Ants)
Environmental Consultants And Dune Restoration
(Glory)
Technical Consultant On Vampire Bats
(Chosen Survivors)
The Cobble Crew (Michael Collins)
Surf Forecaster, Aerial Hair Stylist
(Point Break)
Second Second Assistant Director
(Lolita)
Assistant To The Assistant To The Unit Publicist
(The Greek Tycoon)
Fangs by Dr. Ludwig Von Krankheit
(Dance Of The Vampires)
Catering Cecil B. DeMeals (Cactus)
Visual Effects Crew Fuelled By Michael Smith Of Javva The Hutt
(Star Wars Episode 1: The Phantom Menace)

Only two animals were harmed in the
making of this motion picture.
(State And Main)

This story was based on fact.
Any similiarity with fictional events or characters
is entirely coincidental.
(Slacker)

INDEX

Mu'awiya II (caliph) 22
Muhammad **4–11**
Muhammad Ali 81–2
Muhammad Khodabandeh 63
Muhasibi, al- (mystic) 31
Mulk, Nizam al- 40, 41
Mu'min, 'Abd al- 36
Murad I, Sultan 53–5, 55
Murad II, Sultan 55
Muslim, Abu 26
Muslim Brotherhood **94–5**
Mustaqfi, al- (caliph) 39
Musta'sim, al- (caliph) 49
Mu'tasim, al- (caliph) 32
Mu'tazilite school 30, 31
Mutawakkil (caliph) 39

Nadir Shah 72, 74
Napoleon Bonaparte 81
Nasirid dynasty 36–7
Nasiruddin Shah 86
Nigeria 80, 87
Nizamiyyeh school 40

Nuwas, Abu (poet) 28

OIC 100
Orhan, Sultan 53
Osman 53
Ottoman empire 53–6, 61-2, 63–4, 75–8, **81–5**, 90

Pakistan 91, **95–6**
Palestine 40, 45 *bis*, 86, **92–3**
Pan-Islamic movement 84, 88–9
Persia *see* Iran
Poitiers, battle of 33
Popes 42, 44, 45
Portuguese 64

Qadisiyya, battle of 13
Qara-Qoyunlu dynasty 58, 59
Qays tribe 22, 24
Qizilbash order 59–60, 61

Rahman I, 'Abd al- (emir) 33–4
Rahman II, 'Abd al- (emir) 34
Rahman III, 'Abd al- (caliph) 34
Rajputs 66, 73
Ranjit Singh 74
Rashid al-Din 51
Renaissance 32

Reza Shah 87
Richard the Lionheart 44–5
Russia 49, 77–8, 83–4, 86, 87, 92

Sa'adi (poet) 51–2
Safavid empire 57–8, **69–76**
Saffah, Abu al-'Abbas al- 26
Safi of Ardabil, Shaykh 57
Saladin 39, 44-5
Salafiyya movement 89
Samanid dynasty 38
Samarkand 38, 49, 66
Sanusiyya 80, 88
Sassanid empire 13, 16
Saud, Abdul Aziz ibn 90–1
Saudi Arabia **90–1**
Sebuktegin (caliph) 38
Seljuk dynasty **39–41**, 42, 43
Serbia 54, 55, 77, 82
Shafi'ite school of law 29
shari'a (sacred law) 30, 36, 62
Sher Khan 67
Shi'ism 11–12, 21–2, 25–6, 29–30, 38, 39 *bis*, **57–63**, **70–1**, 79, 86

115

Index

Shivaji (Marathan leader) 73–4
Siffin, battle of 17–18
Sikhs 73, 74
Sinan, Mimar 56
Spain **32–7**
Sudan 80, 87, 88, 91, 98
Suez canal 85
Sufism **30–1**, 41, **57–8**, 79–80
Sufyanids 20
Sulayman (caliph) 24, 26
Sulayman the Magnificent 56, 76
sultan, title of 40
'Sultanate of the Women' 76
Sunnites 11–12, **29–30**, 57
Sykes-Picot agreement 85, 92
Syria 13, 17–18, 44, 81–2, 86, 91

Tabriz 51, 60, 64
Taftazani, Sa'd al-Din 51
Tahmasp, Shah **61–3**
Taj Mahal 68
Talib, Abu 7
Tanzimat reforms 82–3

Tariq b. Ziyad 33
Tatars 52, 78
Taymiyya, Ibn 79, 80
Taymur-i Lang (Timur/Tamburlaine) 52, 54, 66
Timurid dynasty 52–3
trade 47–8, 64, 75–6, 77, 86
'translation movement' 31–2
Treaty of Amasya 61–2
Treaty of Berlin 84
Treaty of Hudaybah 10–11
Treaty of Karlowitz 77
Treaty of Kuchuk Kainarji 78
Treaty of Passarowitz 77
Tulunid dynasty 38
Tumart, Ibn 36
Tunisia 32, 38, 46, 82, 91
Turkey 54, **84–5**, 90; *see also* Ottoman empire
Tusi, Nasir al-Din 50–1

Uhud, battle of 10 *bis*
ulama (scholars) 28, 30–1, 34, **62–3**, **70–1**, 86, 87
Ulugh Beg 51
Umar I (caliph) 12–14, 61
Umar II (caliph) 24–5, 43
Umayyads 15, 17–18, **20–6**, 33–4
United Nations 91, 92, 93
United States of America 93 *bis*
Uthman (caliph) 15–16, 61
Uzbeks 61, 63

Wafd movement 90
Wahhabi movement 78–9, 81
Wali Allah, Shah 79–80
Walid I (caliph) 23, 24
Wathiq, al- (caliph) 32

Yazid I (caliph) 21
Yazid III (caliph) 25
Young Turks movement 84

Zaghloul, Sa'd 90
Zaydi dynasty 38
Zubayr, Abdullah ibn 17, 21, 22–3

their lives and ways were said to be strange and wicked. To him, in the distribution of the dead mother's estate, had fallen all that they deemed of value — the mocking-bird. They could be divided, but it could not, so it was carried away into the strange country, and the world of William knew it no more forever. Yet still through the aftertime of his loneliness its song filled all the dream, and seemed always sounding in his ear and in his heart.

The kinsmen who had adopted the boys were enemies, holding no communication. For a time letters full of boyish bravado and boastful narratives of the new and larger experience — grotesque descriptions of their widening lives and the new worlds they had conquered — passed between them; but these gradually became less frequent, and with William's removal to another and greater city ceased altogether. But ever through it all ran the song of the mocking-bird, and when the dreamer opened his eyes and stared through the vistas of the pine forest the cessation of its music first apprised him that he was awake.

The sun was low and red in the west; the level rays projected from the trunk of each giant pine a wall of shadow traversing the golden haze to eastward until light and shade were blended in undistinguishable blue.

Private Grayrock rose to his feet, looked cautiously about him, shouldered his rifle and set off toward camp. He had gone perhaps a half-mile, and was passing a thicket of laurel, when a bird rose from the midst of it and perching on the branch of a tree above, poured from its joyous breast so inexhaustible floods of song as but one of all God's creatures can utter in His praise. There was little in that — it was only to open the bill and breathe; yet the man stopped as if struck — stopped and let fall his rifle, looked upward at the bird, covered his eyes with his hands and wept like a child! For the moment he was, indeed, a child, in spirit and in memory, dwelling again by the great river, over-against the Enchanted Land! Then with an effort of the will he pulled himself together, picked up his weapon and audibly damning himself for an idiot strode on. Passing an opening that reached into the heart of the little thicket he looked in, and there, supine upon the earth, its arms all abroad, its gray uniform stained with a single spot of blood upon the breast, its white face turned sharply upward and backward, lay the image of himself! — the body of John Grayrock, dead of a gunshot wound, and still warm! He had found his man.

As the unfortunate soldier knelt beside that masterwork of civil war the shrilling bird upon the bough overhead stilled her song and, flushed with sunset's crimson glory, glided silently away through the solemn spaces of the wood. At roll-call that evening in the Federal camp the name William Grayrock brought no response, nor ever again thereafter.

DOVER·THRIFT·EDITIONS

All books complete and unabridged. All 5³⁄₁₆″ × 8¼″, paperbound.
Just $1.00–$2.00 in U.S.A.

A selection of the more than 100 titles in the series:

FLATLAND: A ROMANCE OF MANY DIMENSIONS, Edwin A. Abbott. 96pp. 27263-X $1.00

DOVER BEACH AND OTHER POEMS, Matthew Arnold. 112pp. 28037-3 $1.00

CIVIL WAR STORIES, Ambrose Bierce. 128pp. 28038-1 $1.00

THE DEVIL'S DICTIONARY, Ambrose Bierce. 144pp. 27542-6 $1.00

SONGS OF INNOCENCE AND SONGS OF EXPERIENCE, William Blake. 64pp. 27051-3 $1.00

SONNETS FROM THE PORTUGUESE AND OTHER POEMS, Elizabeth Barrett Browning. 64pp. 27052-1 $1.00

MY LAST DUCHESS AND OTHER POEMS, Robert Browning. 128pp. 27783-6 $1.00

SELECTED POEMS, George Gordon, Lord Byron. 112pp. 27784-4 $1.00

ALICE'S ADVENTURES IN WONDERLAND, Lewis Carroll. 96pp. 27543-4 $1.00

O PIONEERS!, Willa Cather. 128pp. 27785-2 $1.00

THE CHERRY ORCHARD, Anton Chekhov. 64pp. 26682-6 $1.00

THE AWAKENING, Kate Chopin. 128pp. 27786-0 $1.00

THE RIME OF THE ANCIENT MARINER AND OTHER POEMS, Samuel Taylor Coleridge. 80pp. 27266-4 $1.00

HEART OF DARKNESS, Joseph Conrad. 80pp. 26464-5 $1.00

THE RED BADGE OF COURAGE, Stephen Crane. 112pp. 26465-3 $1.00

A CHRISTMAS CAROL, Charles Dickens. 80pp. 26865-9 $1.00

THE CRICKET ON THE HEARTH AND OTHER CHRISTMAS STORIES, Charles Dickens. 128pp. 28039-X $1.00

SELECTED POEMS, Emily Dickinson. 64pp. 26466-1 $1.00

SELECTED POEMS, John Donne. 96pp. 27788-7 $1.00

NOTES FROM THE UNDERGROUND, Fyodor Dostoyevsky. 96pp. 27053-X $1.00

SIX GREAT SHERLOCK HOLMES STORIES, Sir Arthur Conan Doyle. 112pp. 27055-6 $1.00

THE SOULS OF BLACK FOLK, W. E. B. Du Bois. 176pp. 28041-1 $2.00

MEDEA, Euripides. 64pp. 27548-5 $1.00

A BOY'S WILL AND NORTH OF BOSTON, Robert Frost. 112pp. (Available in U.S. only) 26866-7 $1.00

WHERE ANGELS FEAR TO TREAD, E. M. Forster. 128pp. (Available in U.S. only) 27791-7 $1.00

FAUST, PART ONE, Johann Wolfgang von Goethe. 192pp. 28046-2 $2.00

THE SCARLET LETTER, Nathaniel Hawthorne. 192pp. 28048-9 $2.00

A DOLL'S HOUSE, Henrik Ibsen. 80pp. 27062-9 $1.00

THE TURN OF THE SCREW, Henry James. 96pp. 26684-2 $1.00

VOLPONE, Ben Jonson. 112pp. 28049-7 $1.00

DUBLINERS, James Joyce. 160pp. 26870-5 $1.00

A PORTRAIT OF THE ARTIST AS A YOUNG MAN, James Joyce. 192pp. 28050-0 $2.00

LYRIC POEMS, John Keats. 80pp. 26871-3 $1.00

THE BOOK OF PSALMS, King James Bible. 144pp. 27541-8 $1.00

Quellennachweis

S. 9: »Elvis«, von Rainer Bungenstock, mit frdl. Genehmigung des Verf. – S. 13: »Freundschaft«, S. 58: »Logik«, S. 76: ». . . auf die Schulter klopfen«, S. 104: »Einer kommt zum Rebbe« und S. 127: »Ein gemachter Mann«, alle aus: »Der jüdische Witz« von Salcia Landmann, © Walter Verlag AG Olten 1960. – S. 13: »Der Kloß« von Gudrun Pausewang, und S. 92: »Der unbekannte Patient« von Herbert Erdmann, beide aus: »Wunderwelt« – Lesewerk für die Grundschule, 4. Schuljahr, Pädagogischer Verlag Schwann, Düsseldorf. – S. 17: »Ungleiche Boten« von Rudolf Kirsten, aus: »Hundertfünf Fabeln«, Logos-Verlag, Zürich. – S. 18: »Sprechen Sie noch?« von Sigismund von Radecki, aus: »Das ABC des Lachens vom gleichn. Verf., © Rowohlt Verlag GmbH, Hamburg 1953. – S. 19: »Sieh doch!« von Wolfdietrich Schnurre, aus: »Protest im Paterre« vom gleichn. Verf., Albert Langen-Georg Müller Verlag, München. – S. 21: »Der Drachenbauer« von Thomas Valentin, aus: »Rotlicht« vom gleichn. Verf., Signal-Verlag Hans Frevert, Baden-Baden (Signal-Bücherei Bd. 10). – S. 26: »Jesus und die Kinder«, S. 56: »Glauben jenseits der Grenze«, S. 79: »Manchmal gilt: Gott liebt gerade die anderen« und S. 102: ». . . und ging traurig weg« aus: Die Gute Nachricht. Das Neue Testament im heutigen Deutsch, hg. von den Bibelgesellschaften und Bibelwerken im deutschsprachigen Raum, Württembergische Bibelanstalt Stuttgart 1971. – S. 27: »Ein kleiner, bebrillter Ömmes« von Josef Reding und S. 74: »Wächter der Verfassung« von Josef Reding, beide aus: »Wer betet für Judas?« © by Georg Bitter Verlag, Recklinghausen 1958. – S. 31: »Heute hat einer gewinkt (Originaltitel: Die Nacht im Hotel) von Siegfried Lenz, und S. 62: »Ein Haus aus lauter Liebe« von Siegfried Lenz, beide aus: JÄGER DES SPOTTS, Geschichten aus dieser Zeit, © Hoffmann und Campe Verlag, Hamburg 1958. – S. 35: »Keine Zeit«, aus: Wochenschau für politische Erziehung, Sozial- und Gemeinschaftskunde Nr. 10, Ausgabe U Juni 1974, Wochenschau-Verlag Dr. Debus & Co., Schwalbach Limes. – S. 37: »In bester Gesellschaft« von Guy Abecassis, aus: »100 Koffer auf dem Dach. Auf Gesellschaftsreisen vom Nordkap bis Kairo. Ein Reiseleiter plaudert aus dem Busch, Agence Hoffman, München. – S. 40: »Unter dem Strich« von Dorothee Zimmermann, aus: contrapunkt Nr. 5, Sept. 1972, Evangelische Zeitschrift für die junge Generation im MKB-Verlag, Bad Salzuflen. – S. 41: »Henry Adams« von Archibald Joseph Cronin, aus: »Abenteuer in zwei Welten« vom gleichn. Verf., deutsche Rechte MOHRBOOKS, Zürich. – S. 51: »Medizin ohne Menschlichkeit«, aus dem gleichn. Buch, hg. und kommentiert von A. Mitscherlich und F. Mielke, © 1949 by Verlag Lambert Schneider, Heidelberg, Abdruck mit Genehmigung des Fischer Taschenbuchverlags, Frankfurt a. M. – S. 55: »Er lag in einem Torfbett« von Friedrich von Bodelschwingh, mit frdl. Genehmigung des Verf. – S. 59: »Hau ab, Zigeuner« (Originaltitel: War José anders?) von Mauro Pellegrini, Publiz. Büro Dr. P. Herzog, Tübingen. – S. 72: »Vierbeiner gut, Zweibeiner besser!« von George Orwell aus »Farm der Tiere« vom gleichn. Verf., Graphis Verlag Walter Herdeg, Zürich. – S. 77: »Würden Sie das für alle Afrikaner sagen?«, aus dem Film FT 2423 »Mama und Papa« FWV, Institut für Film und Bild in Wissenschaft und Unterricht. Grünwald/München. – S. 79: »Schischyphusch oder der Kellner meines Onkels«

von Wolfgang Borchert, aus: Wolfgang Borchert: DAS GESAMTWERK, © Rowohlt Verlag GmbH, Hamburg 1949. – S. 95: »Lernziel erreicht?« von Ingrid Engel, mit frdl. Genehmigung der Verf. – S. 96: »Nur die Brieftasche« von Thomas Valentin, aus: »Die Unberatenen« vom gleichn. Verfasser, Copyright © 1968 by Claassen Verlag, Hamburg und Düsseldorf. – S. 97: »Kauf dir das Lied, das die Nachtigall singt« von Mischa Mleinek, aus: Ulrich Beer: »Konsumerziehung gegen Konsumzwang«, Katzmann-Verlag, Tübingen 1974 (3. Aufl.). – S. 98: »Der Tod der Elsa Baskoleit« von Heinrich Böll, und S. 106: »Genug zum Leben« (Originaltitel: Anekdote zur Senkung der Arbeitsmoral) von Heinrich Böll, beide aus: »Erzählungen 1950–1970« von Heinrich Böll, © 1972 by Verlag Kiepenheuer & Witsch, Köln. – S. 105: »Der gekränkte Badegast« von Eugen Roth, aus: »Ein Mensch« vom gleichn. Verf., Carl Hanser Verlag, München. – S. 106: »Schade, daß wir keine Peruaner sind« von Walther Lehmann, Verlag Junge Stimme, Stuttgart. – S. 110: »Wenn ich erwachsen sein werde, aus: »RELIGION: Standpunkte« 7/10 Hauptschule, hg. von H.-D. Bastian, H. Rauschenberger, D. Stoodt und Kl. Wegenast, Pro Schule Verlag, Düsseldorf 1974. – S. 112: »Die Mahnung des Betriebsratsvorsitzenden« von Gerd Sowka, mit frdl. Genehmigung des Verf. – S. 114: »Die fremde Gerechtigkeit«, aus: Das Neue Testament. Übertragen von Jörg Zink. Kreuz-Verlag, Stuttgart und Berlin. – S. 116: »Ich bin nur ein Fabrikmädchen«, aus dem Film FT 2363 »Mama und Papa – Afrikaner als Untermieter«, FWU, Institut für Film und Bild in Wissenschaft und Unterricht, Grünwald, München. – S. 119: »Der silberne Schuh« (Originaltitel: Leistungen) von Theo Schmich, copyright by ruhr-story, Gelsenkirchen-Buer. S. 120: »Die Enttäuschung« von Kurt Rommel, mit frdl. Genehmigung des Verf. – S. 123: »Birne besucht die Olympiade« von Günter Herburger, aus: BIRNE KANN NOCH MEHR, vom gleichn. Verf., © 1971 by Hermann Luchterhand Verlag, Darmstadt und Neuwied.
Folgende Texte sind von Weert Flemmig und Hans-Heinrich Strube verfaßt: S. 10: »Wer angibt, hat mehr vom Leben«; S. 16: Texte zu den Gedankenblasen »Wer ist ein Kumpel . . .?«; S. 40: »Worauf kommt es an?«; S. 50: »Was ist ein Mensch wert?«; S. 54: »Verrechnet und verschoben«; S. 71/71: »Schlag-Wörter«; S. 103: »Macht Moneten, Männer!« und S. 117: »Ich bin nur ein Fabrikmädchen (2. Teil).
Die Reproduktion der Karikatur von Peter Neugebauer auf S. 73 erfolgte mit frdl. Genehmigung der Redaktion STERN (STERN Nr. 49/73).

1. Why was Mr. Heatherstone surprised?
2. What must Edward arrange to do?
3. "Her —— soon changed to ——"

21.
1. What did Edward learn?
2. "They must —— here, and work like ——" What must the girls do?
3. What did Edward know?
1. Where was Humphrey working?
2. What did Edward show the soldiers?
3. Why did the soldiers go to the sea-coast?
1. What was granted to the Intendant?
2. What did the Intendant doubt?
3. What did Benjamin give to Mr. Heatherstone?
1. "Now I shall never be ——" What?
2. "Some day I hope that ——" What?
3. What will the Government never know?
1. What could Edward offer Patience?
2. "If the King ——, I must —— with him in ——" What did Edward say?
3. What was Patience doing?

22.
1. What did Edward show Alice?
2. Who were Edith's friends, too?
3. What did Humphrey buy in Lymington?
4. What did they sail in?
1. Where did the girls live?
2. What did Edward become?
3. What did the French make King Charles do?
1. What did the ladies wave?
2. What did the two girls do in the forest?
3. What must the girls show the King's French friends?
4. Who was the most beautiful woman in London?
1. Why did Edward receive no reply to his letters?
2. What did King Charles do that evening?
3. What was Edward's duty?
4. What did Edward know when Patience smiled?
1. What did Edward give to Humphrey?
2. Whom did Humphrey marry?

Pronunciation of the chief names of persons and places

The pronunciation given is the system used in The International Phonetic Alphabet.

Armitage	ˈaamitidʒ
Arnwood	ˈaanwud
Barnet	ˈbaanit
Benjamin	ˈbendʒəmin
Bolton	ˈboultən
Captain Marryat	ˈkæptin ˈmæriət
Chaloner	ˈtʃælənə
Clara	ˈkleərə
Colonel Beverley	ˈkəənəl ˈbevəli
Corbould	ˈkɔɔbould
Cromwell	krɔmwəl
Cunningham	ˈkʌniŋhəm
(Lord) Derby	ˈdaabi
Grenville	ˈgrenvil
Heatherstone	ˈheðəstoun
Holland	ˈhɔlənd
Humphrey	ˈhʌmfri
Hurst	həəst
(The) Intendant	inˈtendənt
Isle of Wight	ail əv wait
Jacob (Armitage)	ˈdʒeikəb
James Southwold	ˈdʒeimz ˈsauθwould
Judith Villiers	ˈdʒuudiθ ˈviliəz
Lambert	ˈlæmbət
Langton	ˈlæŋtən
Lymington	ˈlimiŋtən
Middleton	ˈmidltən
Naseby	ˈneizbi
Oswald Partridge	ˈɔzwəld ˈpaatridʒ
Patience (Heather-stone)	ˈpeiʃəns
Portlake	ˈpɔɔtleik
Ratcliff	ˈrætklif
Samson	ˈsæmsən
Spain	spein
Warrington	ˈwɔriŋtən
Wigan	ˈwigən
Worcester	ˈwustə
York	iɔɔk

Det är höst och skymmer tidigt på.

Joel går i skogen, bryter kvistar, snubblar i ris. Men nu har han haft tårar i ögonen.

Ett ögonblick har han varit uppe i kojan. Rå, död kyla därinne, tidningarna fuktfläckiga och klibbiga. En kullvält ljusstump på golvet. Han brydde sig inte om att tända den.

Går vidare, ensam, oåterkalleligt ensam, med bilden av en flicka inom sig, av ett långt hår och lugna, grå ögon.

Allt det andra kan gå an. Men att hon är borta. Så helt borta, fastän levande och densamma.

Och han minns mest: Lenas huvud i hans knä. Lenas smala axlar och tysta gråt. Hon visste.

Skriva tänker inte Joel på. Brevens tid och möjligheter är ännu inte komna för honom. Och brev hade ändå inte kunnat överbrygga avståndet.

Den stora närheten kan aldrig återställas, krympas kanske, men inte bli densamma. Aldrig.

Åren förändrar, innebär mycket nytt, rycker en med sig. Man är inte densamma det ena året som det andra.

Lena kan han kanske träffa igen, men en annan Lena än lilla syster.

Nu ska hon förbli lilla syster inom honom, evigt orörd av år och händelser, evigt följa honom sådan hon var den sommaren. Något har börjat. Något har slutat.

Livet väntar, men dock: detta ska vara med som en del av detta okända, oöverskådliga liv. Det kan aldrig tvättas ur, kanske blekna, sjunka undan, men inte utplånas.

Ja, stackars den som får sitta ensam på ett fall när tranorna flyttar.

Lena grät när han sa det.

I vår, då kommer tranorna tillbaks. Och på fallet ska han vara då, och se, om inte en av dem ser ner på honom. Och liknar Lena.

Nu känner Joel värme genom den inre förlamningen. Men han hade i alla fall, en gång, en liten syster. Hon fanns, och fastän tomheten efter henne skulle bli lång skulle dock lika länge minnets rikedom finnas kvar.

Bilderna från den sommaren, innan de första höstlöven föll.

The new, revolutionary, quick, easy and *safe* Tom Topper way to drive is winning friends the world over. Wonderful reviews appeared on publication and here are some extracts:

> *The Times:* 'Down-to-earth ... practical ... basic.'
> *Daily Telegraph:* 'For those who are still struggling ... good value.'
> *Daily Mirror:* 'Clearer than many more expensive manuals.'
> *The Sun:* 'Admirable ... amazingly cheap ... invaluable.'
> *Daily Sketch:* 'Easiest to understand ... excellent.'
> *Woman's Own:* 'Very helpful ... gives all the theory.'

The book carries our famous 'Test Pass Guarantee' or return for refund.

Tom Topper is also author of **VERY ADVANCED DRIVING** – a bombshell upon established thinking. Some reviews:
Daily Mail: '... has some very advanced thinking indeed ...'
Motor Sport: '... packed full of driving hints suitably diagrammed ... could do a great deal of good ...'
(Burton) Daily Mail: '... Through and through Tom Topper sticks relentlessly, and with clarity, to showing his readers the techniques they can use and build on. He deals with the problems that confront drivers day in, day out ... This book will shake the motoring world by its roots ...'

Both books uniform with this one

Remember, if a subject in which you are interested is not mentioned, simply write for our free catalogue which we will be delighted to send; Paperfronts cover many other subjects:

ELLIOT PAPERFRONTS, Kingswood, Surrey, U.K.

EASYMADE WINE AND COUNTRY DRINKS

by Mrs. Gennery Taylor

Simplicity : Economy : Wine fit for a Queen! Many do not realize that wine-making can be continued all the year round. This book contains a comprehensive Wine Calendar. Intended for the ordinary housewife or husband, simple instructions show how to make a delightful variety of wines for a few pence per bottle.

Times Literary Supplement '... simpler than most, is informally written, calls for very little special apparatus...'

Birmingham Evening Mail '... simple, straightforward, economical – and great fun, both for its recipes and its cheeky little cartoon illustrations.'

Uniform with this book

Also published in the wonderful PAPERFRONT *series:*

COCKTAIL PARTY SECRETS

by Vernon Heaton

Make it a roaring success! Big Parties : Little Parties : 'Cocktails' : 'Drinks' : 'At Homes'

Uniform with this book

Teyler-processen 50
Teylers Stichting 50
theogonie 10
thesaurier 121
tienjaren (-jaarlijkse) tafels 74
toevalsvondst 124
Toll, Jurriaan van 28
transporten 119
Trente (Concilie van) 80, 98
Trinity Church 51v
Troje 11, 12
trouwboekjes 63
trouwen (in geboorte- of woonplaats bruid) 84
tijdrekenkunde 103v

Uerdingen 106
uiterlijk (beschrijving van) 108
Utah 56
Utrecht (prov.) 114

Valkenburg, C. C. van 40
Veendam 22
Verenigde Staten, zie Amerika
verhuurcontracten 118
verticale schikking 64
Verwandschaftstafel 68
verwantschap (geestelijke) 99
Verwijs, E. 41, 42
verzoekschriften 118
vete of vede 11
vinding (akte van) 97
Vink, A. K. 31
Vlaams Centrum voor Genealogie en Heraldiek 38
Vlaamse Stam (tijdschrift) 35, 45, 92, 107, 109, 114, 118, 123
Vlaamse Vereniging voor Familiekunde (VVF) 8, 24, 35v, 44, 45, 69, 92, 102, 110, 123, 126
Vlaanderen 24, 44
volkenkunde 56

volksverhalen 62
Vollenhoven, M. W. R. van 63
volmachten 118
vondelingen 97v
vondelingen-molen 97
voogden 119
voorouderverering 10
Vorsterman van Oyen, Anthonie Abraham 19, 20, 22, 92
Vosburg (familie) 111
vroedschap (resolutiën v.d.) 119
vrijwillige rechtspraak 119
Vulsma, R. F. 67
Waalse kerken 100
Wagner, Richard 55
Wanneperveen 82
wapenboeken 44
wapenborden 44
weeskamer 119
Westerveld, J. 47
Wildeman, M. G. 23
Wilden Boer, Paulus den 119
Willem III (koning) 40
Willemsz., Willem 50
Willige Langerak 119
Winkler, Johan 42
Wolters (collectie) 107
Wijnaends van Resandt, W. 81, 89, 104, 111, 114
Wijnen, R. A. 64

Zabrisky, Olin 53
Zeeland 114
Zeeuws-Vlaanderen 74, 76
Zentrallstelle für Deutsche Personen- und Familiengeschichte 23, 33
zoen 12
Zuid-Holland 114
zwaard- en spillezijde 11
zwagerschapstabel 68
Zwitserland 113

143

choix de leurs activités de détente : ils jouent au squash pour se reposer de la vie trépidante que leur impose leur travail, lancent des motos à toute vitesse pour oublier les embouteillages, tirent sur des extenseurs pour se délasser du maniement du balai !

D'autres n'ont pas les moyens de tels agissements. Ils ont moins de vingt-cinq ans et n'ont pas pu trouver d'emploi à la sortie de l'école ; plus de cinquante et ils ont découvert, le jour où l'entreprise qui les employait a fait faillite, qu'ils étaient « trop vieux » pour prétendre refaire leur vie professionnelle. Ils ont n'importe quel âge et ils ont « le temps de vivre », mais le goût leur en a passé. Ils sont chômeurs, parfois délinquants, punks ou clochards. Ils traînent leur ennui sur les pavés d'une société qui n'a pas de place pour eux. Ils ont retrouvé, à leur manière, le poids de l'oisiveté des salons de l'Ancien Régime tel que le dénonçait Rivarol par ces mots : « Quand la fortune nous exempte de travail, la nature nous accable du temps » !

Le problème est donc bien plus complexe que ne semble l'affirmer Guéhenno : notre société procure, en effet, plus de « temps libre » que celle d'autrefois... mais ce n'est guère une « chance » pour ceux qui en bénéficient à longueur de journée. Pour les autres, le rythme est comparable à celui qu'a connu la « mère aux abois » qu'il évoque, mais ce rythme comporte, outre le travail, une part non négligeable de loisirs, bien souvent aussi échevelés que le reste de l'existence... Sans doute ceux qui les pratiquent refusent-ils de prendre conscience de la part de responsabilité qui leur incombe et se plaindront-ils, au cours de leur « jogging », de la fatigue qui les poursuit. Mais le mal n'est peut-être pas si récent qu'il peut le paraître ; La Bruyère ne déclarait-il pas déjà : « Ceux qui emploient mal leur temps sont les premiers à se plaindre de sa brièveté » ?

Aubin Imprimeur
LIGUGÉ, POITIERS

Photocomposition : Imprimerie Bussière
Achevé d'imprimer en août 1987
N° d'édition 5196 / N° d'impression L 25230
Dépôt légal, août 1987
Imprimé en France

the safe and loved girls our ages? What did we do to be brought here to this place?

At the bottom of the stairway, they waited for me to catch up.

"Stick close," Brooke ordered. "You're one of us now."

"I think I've always been," I muttered.

Brooke smiled.

Butterfly looked sad.

Crystal looked thoughtful.

We continued down the hallway, together. Four of us closing ranks, hardening, gathering the strength with which to do battle against loneliness.

Firing up our precious star.

XAVIER

She ate and loved giving her apple. What did we do to be brought here to this place?

At the bottom of the stairway, they waited for me to catch up.

"Stick close," Brooke ordered, "you're meant to live."

"I think I've always been," I muttered.

Brooke smiled.

Butterfly looked sad.

Crystal looked thoughtful.

We continued down the hallway together. Four of us closing ranks, hardening, gathering the strength with which to do battle against loneliness. Filling up our precious star.

Report on the Heights & Weights Of School Pupils in . . . 1959, 100
respectability, 6, 10, 140
Rimmel, 67
river frontage, 4
romantic comics, 81
room-lets, 3
rootlessness, 35
Round About a Pound a Week, ix, 3, 11
Roupell Street, 20
Rowlands, Marjorie, 47–48, 53, 72, 117, 120, 123, 132, 133, 134
Royal Waterloo Hospital for Women & Children, 2

St George's RC Cathedral, 5
St George's Road, 48
St Saviour's Salamanca, 51
St Thomas's Hospital, 98
Salvation Army, 97
Sarsons', 8
scent, 68
school, 52, 58
School Health Service Reports, 101
school meals, 106
School Medical Officer, 99, 100
school milk, 106
Schweppes shelter, 77
Sealy, Mary, 145
Sealy, Mr, 145
seasonal work, 19, 56, 113
separation, 108
sex education, lack of, 88
sexual knowledge, 88
Shaftesbury Hall, 98
Shell Centre, 135
shoes, 50
shop girls, 65
shopping, 113, 131, 132, 133, 134, 137, 146
shopping precincts, 135
single parents, 83, 106, 107
Slater & Woodside, 89, 107
skipping, 47
slimming, 70
smocks, 25
solicitors, 32
soup kitchens, 98
South Bank, 2
South London music-hall, 26
South London Press, 6
South-Western Railway Company, 2, 3

Southwark, 1
Southwark Park, 153
Springer, Maude, 21, 26, 98
Spurgeon's Tabernacle, 6
stairs, 15, 16, 21, 29
stall-holders, 22
standards: 10, 16, 18, 21, 30, 50, 51, 169
nutrition, 99
Stangate Buildings, 3
Stebbing system, 70
Stebbings, Debbie, 35, 156
stenographers, 65
stillbirths, 105
stockings, 68
Stones, 127
street names, 4
stress, 109
sub-letting, 3, 18, 114
Sunbeams, 98
Sunday dinners, 26
Sunday School, 45
supermarkets, 134–38, 146
supervisors, 29
supplementary benefit, 102
Surrey music-hall, 26
swearing, 63
sweets, 27
Swinnock, Mr, 43

tailor's runner, 64
tally men, 118, 121
Tarbuck, Gracie, 46, 64, 89, 97, 129, 130
Teddy boys, 79
teenagers, 80, 81
telephone, 124
television, 34
Telford, Carrie, 20, 27, 64, 133
tenant rights, 169
tenants' associations, 31, 35
tenements, 3, 14
Tennison Street, 30
tension, 109
Terry, Ada, 17, 27, 37, 39, 40, 68, 71, 74, 98, 99, 116
Tesco's, 134
Thede Street, 20
Thomas, Queenie, 17, 19, 22, 40, 47, 49, 51, 52, 63, 69, 71, 86, 119
Thorpe, Maggie, 35, 59, 138, 150
thrift club, 121
Titbits, 65, 67, 70
tot stalls, 114, 128

Townsend, Peter, 104
trades, 4
Tramways Department, 4
transistor radios, 80
Twist, 118
Tyer's Street, 129

underwear, 39, 50
unemployment: 7, 9, 23, 96, 100, 102, 104, 143
   women, 9
United States National Research Council, 103
Upper Marsh, 4

Vauxhall, 8, 17, 35, 43
Vauxhall Street, 129

wages, 76
Walcot Estate, 4, 6
Walworth Road Registry Office, 74
wash-house, 124
washing, 45, 47, 95, 113, 124
   copper, 15, 16
   lavatories, 15, 17
   stairs, 15, 16, 21, 29
   wash-house, 15
washing day, 24
Waterloo, 8, 16, 20, 29
Waterloo Church gardens, 20
Waterloo District Plan, 2

Waterloo Station, 2
Waxwell Terrace, 19
wedding-ring, 117
weddings, 73, 81, 82, 147
weekly men, 118
weight, 99, 100, 106
Weldon's Home Dressmaker, 67, 70
Welfare State, 58, 79, 100
West, Karen, 32, 59, 147
West Indians, 107, 140, 143
Westminster, 7
Westminster College, 167
Whit Sunday, 115
White, Lily, 24, 38, 66, 114
'white curtain streets', 20
Whittlesea Street, 20
wife-battering, 75
Wincarnis tonic, 70
winkles, 40
wireless, 2, 76
women, 9
Woolworth's, 67, 134
workhouse, 5
Workhouse Infirmary, 92
working, 62–65
World War II, 6, 54, 76, 77

York Road, 4
youth clubs, 35

Zaïre, 163

If you do decide to develop your self-defence techniques by joining a martial arts club:

* Make sure you can take the discipline. It is rigorous work which requires not only enthusiasm but also great personal control. It is a disciplined training of a formal range of sports. There is no room for prima donnas and the inflated egos of football stars.

* Make sure you can afford it. Club fees, equipment and travelling expenses all add up. Check you have enough money to see you through what is effectively a 'lifetime' of training, from first steps to black belt.

* Stick at it. You will learn very slowly. Like all complex subjects and skills, it takes time and experience to master a martial art. It is not something for a one-term evening school course, like Beginners' French. The benefits of martial arts are long-term and there can be no rush to perfection.

* Join a reputable club. Check that the club you are thinking of joining is a member of one of the governing associations. In Britain, these include the British Judo Association, the Amateur Judo Association, British Karate Federation, National Karate Federation of Great Britain, British Ju-Jitsu Association, British Aikido Association, British Kendo Association and British Kung Foo Association. If in doubt, check with the national association, which will always put you right.

* Ask yourself if you are fit enough! There is a lot of tumble (if not rough) in martial arts and though it will improve your fitness, you do have to be mobile to find the training of any value. If you are frail or old, think hard – and remind yourself that there is still much you can do to ensure your personal safety even without martial art skills.

If you do go ahead, I wish you every success. But remember always: young, old, frail or tough – the best way to beat trouble is still to avoid it. If there has been one vital lesson in this book, that is it.

Telvista Television Company have commenced production of a series of video tapes based on *Fighting Back* which will be available by the end of 1983.

I chatther, chatther as I flow
To join the brimming river,
For men may come and men may go,
But I go on for ever.

Well, he'd learned poethry and had kissed a girl. If he hadn' gone to school, he'd met the scholars; if he hadn' gone into the house, he had knocked at the door.

'A most beautiful and sweet country as any under Heaven' – EDMUND SPENSER

'Put an Irishman on the spit, and you can always get another Irishman to turn him – GEORGE BERNARD SHAW

Whatever your view of Ireland you'll delight in these magnificent authors.

FISH FOR FRIDAY & Other Stories	Frank O'Connor	25p
MY FATHER'S SON (illus.)	Frank O'Connor	30p
THE MAD LOMASNEYS & Other Stories (Selected from Collection Two)	Frank O'Connor	25p
AN ONLY CHILD	Frank O'Connor	30p
AUTOBIOGRAPHY Volume 1: I KNOCK AT THE DOOR	Sean O'Casey	30p
AUTOBIOGRAPHY Volume 2: PICTURES IN THE HALLWAY	Sean O'Casey	30p
THE HEAT OF THE SUN	Sean O'Faolain	30p
THE FLIGHT OF THE DOVES (illus.)	Walter Macken	20p
SEEK THE FAIR LAND	Walter Macken	30p
THE SILENT PEOPLE	Walter Macken	30p
BROWN LORD OF THE MOUNTAIN	Walter Macken	30p
THE SCORCHING WIND	Walter Macken	30p
RAIN ON THE WIND	Walter Macken	30p
A TASTE OF IRELAND (illus.)	Theodora Fitz-gibbon	60p

Postscript

the barren fields for crumbs of food. Here too was the cruel eviction scene described above which supplied the frame for the whole plot. All these things were true.

But I still wanted a happy ending. In the classic ghost story, order is restored only when the troubled dead are in some way comforted. This happens in *Black Harvest* and it is the three children who, having suffered with the famine people, resolve their unquiet and give them their rest. That is why my final image is the biblical one of the rainbow, not a weapon of war but a promise of peace.

Black Harvest was my first published book but, although I have written many since, it is the book with which, to quote Vita Sackville-West, I am "the least dissatisfied". When I wrote it I knew nothing about rules, about "ideal lengths", about "levels of vocabulary". I wrote it in my own way, exactly as it came to me, with an intense, ever-increasing involvement until, in the end, I became my own characters.

The day I finished it I went to visit my next-door neighbour who said, "Goodness, Ann, you're so pale! You look as if you've seen a ghost."

I remember my answer as I sank into a chair. "I've just finished my book about the Irish Famine. Could I possibly have a cup of tea with you?" Because, you see, it was hard to separate myself from the people who had lived with me so long.

Postscript

A storyteller's first aim should surely be to deliver a good read, but I'd like to think *Black Harvest* might also enlarge the sympathies and understanding of those who turn its pages. If it does it will, in its own dark way, have achieved what Robert Frost said a good poem can do, which is to "begin in delight and end in wisdom".

ANN PILLING

'I had arranged that with them beforehand,' Shayne explained easily. 'I thought I'd get a rise out of Bryant that way. Up to that time I didn't have any proof that Bryant was interested in seeing Carson inherit the mine.'

'But, how did you get them to co-operate with you?'

'That was easy.' Shayne took a meditative sip of his cognac. 'I appealed to their greed. You see, *they* thought Pete was Dalcor and were afraid his third would revert to Frank Carson. So they were anxious to play ball when I suggested that we deny the existence of the evidence.'

'But that was downright crooked of them if they didn't know the truth when they agreed with you.'

Shayne assented gravely. 'That's right, Phyl. In their greedy desire to keep all of the mine for themselves they played right into my hands.'

'I didn't hear either one of them even thank you after it was all over. And if it hadn't been for you no one would ever have known the truth, and Carson might have gotten Pete's share of the mine.' Phyllis' voice held righteous indignation though slightly muffled as she vigorously towelled her face and neck.

Shayne said, 'One doesn't expect thanks.' He touched the breast pocket of his coat holding a deed to a tenth interest in the mine. He grinned to himself and continued, 'One's reward comes from a sense of civic duty well performed. You've taught me that, Phyl. The-ah-dignity of my profession as opposed to the sordid and mercenary outlook I used to have before you came into my life.'

'What did you say?'

'I was just saying——'

She advanced upon him swiftly, swathed in a heavy robe, and settled herself on his lap. 'I heard you,' she laughed. 'You're wonderful and I adore you, but—I don't want to change you too much, Michael. It wouldn't be so hot if you let yourself get in the habit of not collecting fees.'

Shayne pulled her face down and kissed her lips. He promised, 'We'll struggle along somehow. There's generally a dollar or so to be picked up if a man knows where to look for it.'

We all crowded round Poirot asking questions, elucidating this point and that.

"Those questions, Poirot? That you asked of everybody. Was there any point in them?"

"Some of them were *simplement une blague*. But I learnt one thing that I wanted to know—*that Franklin Clarke was in London when the first letter was posted*—and also I wanted to see his face when I asked my question of Mademoiselle Thora. He was off his guard. I saw all the malice and anger in his eyes."

"You hardly spared my feelings," said Thora Grey.

"I do not fancy you returned me a truthful answer, mademoiselle," said Poirot dryly. "And now your second expectation is disappointed. Franklin Clarke will not inherit his brother's money."

She flung up her head.

"Is there any need for me to stay here and be insulted?"

"None whatever," said Poirot and held the door open politely for her.

"That fingerprint clinched things, Poirot," I said thoughtfully. "He went all to pieces when you mentioned that."

"Yes, they are useful—fingerprints."

He added thoughtfully:

"I put that in to please you, my friend."

"But, Poirot," I cried, "wasn't it *true*?"

"Not in the least, *mon ami*," said Hercule Poirot.

I must mention a visit we had from Mr. Alexander Bonaparte Cust a few days later. After wringing Poirot's hand and endeavouring very incoherently and unsuccessfully to thank him, Mr. Cust drew himself up and said:

"Do you know, a newspaper has actually offered me a hundred pounds—*a hundred pounds*—for a brief account of my life and history. I—I really don't know what to do about it."

"I should not accept a hundred," said Poirot. "Be firm. Say five hundred is your price. And do not confine yourself to one newspaper."

"Do you really think—that I might——"

"You must realise," said Poirot smiling, "that you are

a very famous man. Practically the most famous man in England to-day."

Mr. Cust drew himself up still further. A beam of delight irradiated his face.

"Do you know, I believe you're right! Famous! In all the papers. I shall take your advice, M. Poirot. The money will be most agreeable—most agreeable. I shall have a little holiday . . . And then I want to give a nice wedding present to Lily Marbury—a dear girl—really a dear girl, M. Poirot."

Poirot patted him encouragingly on the shoulder.

"You are quite right. Enjoy yourself. And—just a little word—what about a visit to an oculist. Those headaches, it is probably that you want new glasses."

"You think that it may have been that all the time?"

"I do."

Mr. Cust shook him warmly by the hand.

"You're a very great man, M. Poirot."

Poirot, as usual, did not disdain the compliment. He did not even succeed in looking modest.

When Mr. Cust had strutted importantly out, my old friend smiled across at me.

"So, Hastings—we went hunting once more, did we not? *Vive le sport.*"

THE END

to face the pain of parting all over again. How could she bear it?

The music came to an end and Florence began to let Archie go but, to her surprise, he continued to hold her tightly.

"Do you want another dance?" she enquired, glancing up at him.

The expression on his face made her heart race and her temperature rise. He was looking down at her with such intensity and passion that she could barely breathe.

"I don't want another dance," he told her huskily. "I want much more than that."

Florence held her breath.

"I don't want to let you go ever again!" he said, his eyes full of fire. "I love you. I've never stopped loving you! I was a fool to let you go.

"Flo, my darling Flo, please tell me you can find it in your heart to forgive me. That we can try again."

Tears filled her eyes and she swallowed hard.

"Of course we can, Archie. There is nothing to forgive."

"You think you might be able to love me again?" he faltered, his face filling with hope and joy.

"I never stopped."

For a moment he stared down at her, a smile of pure happiness transforming his face. Then he pulled her closer and kissed her long and hard.

Florence returned his kiss, her fingers entwined in his hair and, for the first time in over two years, she felt entirely happy.

She was complete again at last.

The End.

DC THOMSON MEDIA

Published in Great Britain by DC Thomson & Co. Ltd., Dundee, Glasgow and London. Distributed by Frontline Ltd, Stuart House, St John's St, Peterborough, Cambridgeshire PE1 5DD. Tel: +44 (0) 1733 555161. Website: www.frontlinedistribution.co.uk EXPORT DISTRIBUTION (excluding AU and NZ) Seymour Distribution Ltd, 2 East Poultry Avenue, London EC1A 9PT. Tel: +44(0)20 7429 4000. Fax: +44(0)20 7429 4001. Email: info@seymour.co.uk. Website: www.seymour.co.uk. EU Representative Office: DC Thomson & Co Ltd, c/o Findmypast Ireland, Irishtown, Athlone, Co. Westmeath, N37 XP52

© DC Thomson & Co. Ltd., and Katie Ashmore, 2022.

We are committed to journalism of the highest standards and abide by the Editors' Code of Practice which is enforced by the Independent Press Standards Organisation (IPSO). If you have a complaint, you can e-mail us at Readerseditor@dcthomson.co.uk or write to the Readers' Editor at The People's Friend, DC Thomson & Co. Ltd., 2 Albert Square, Dundee DD1 9QJ.

(ipso) Regulated

DON'T MISS THE NEXT POCKET NOVEL NO. 966, ON SALE MAY 26, 2022.

IF YOU ARE LOOKING FOR BACK NUMBERS PLEASE TELEPHONE 0800 318846

Select Bibliography

Picard, Liza, *Shakespeare's London: Everyday Life in Elizabethan London*. London: Orion Books, 2003

Piper, David, *O Sweet Mr. Shakespeare I'll Have His Picture: The Changing Image of Shakespeare's Person, 1600–1800*. London: National Portrait Gallery, 1964

Rosenbaum, Ron, *The Shakespeare Wars: Clashing Scholars, Public Fiascoes, Palace Coups*. New York: Random House, 2006

Rowse, A.L., *Shakespeare's Southampton: Patron of Virginia*. London: Macmillan, 1965

Schoenbaum, S., *William Shakespeare: A Documentary Life*. Oxford: Oxford University Press, 1975

_____, *Shakespeare's Lives*. Oxford: Oxford University Press, 1993

Shapiro, James, *1599: A Year in the Life of William Shakespeare*. London: Faber & Faber, 2005

Spevack, Marvin, *The Harvard Concordance to Shakespeare*. Cambridge, Mass.: Belknap Press/Harvard University Press, 1973

Spurgeon, Caroline F.E., *Shakespeare's Imagery and What it Tells Us*. Cambridge: Cambridge University Press, 1935

Starkey, David, *Elizabeth: The Struggle for the Throne*. London: HarperCollins, 2001

Thomas, David, *Shakespeare in the Public Records*. London: HMSO, 1985

Thurley, Simon, *Hampton Court: A Social and Architectural History*. New Haven: Yale University Press, 2003

Vendler, Helen, *The Art of Shakespeare's Sonnets*. Cambridge, Mass.: Belknap Press/Harvard University Press, 1999

SHAKESPEARE

Wells, Stanley, *Shakespeare for All Time*. London: Macmillan, 2002

―――, *Shakespeare & Co.: Christopher Marlowe, Thomas Dekker, Ben Jonson, Thomas Middleton, John Fletcher and the Other Players in His Story*. London: Penguin/Allen Lane, 2006

――― and Paul Edmondson, *Shakespeare's Sonnets*. Oxford: Oxford University Press, 2004

――― and Gary Taylor (eds), *The Oxford Shakespeare: The Complete Works*. Oxford: Clarendon Press, 1994

Wolfe, Heather (ed.), *'The Pen's Excellencie': Treasures from the Manuscript Collection of the Folger Shakespeare Library*. Washington, D.C.: Folger Library Publications, 2002

Youings, Joyce, *Sixteenth Century England*. London: Penguin, 1984

Index

Shakespeare, William, 35–36, 55, 57
Shattuck, Roger, 119
shopping malls, 13, 103, 104, 154
Silvers, Robert, 115, 117–19, 120, 121
Simon & Schuster, 89–90
    editorial staff at, 7
    online distribution explored by, 22–23
    online publishing effort of, 24, 30, 34
    ownership of, 11
    returns accepted by, 95–96
    sales levels of, 100
Sister Carrie (Dreiser), 69–70, 79
socialism, 151
South Africa, CIA-sponsored students from, 123–24
Southern, Terry, 5–6
Soviet Union:
    collapse of, 76, 77
    samizdat writers of, 173, 174
    U.S. Cold War views of, 112, 113, 118, 122–23
Spellman, Francis Joseph Cardinal, 5
spitting, 98
Stalinism, 112–13, 114
Steel, Danielle, 33
Stein, Gertrude, 93, 101
Stendhal (Marie-Henri Beyle), 47
Stevens, Wallace, 17, 93
Stevenson, Adlai, 63
storytellers, technologies of, xvii–xxi, 108–9

Strange Death of Liberal England, The (Dangerfield), viii
Strayhorn, Billy, 63
Strouse, Jean, 14–16
Styron, William, xv, 43–44, 189
subscription sales, 95, 142, 169–71
suburban migration, 13, 102, 103, 104, 105, 148
Supreme Court, U.S., on literary censorship, 74, 78, 81
Swenson, Arnold, 64

Tattered Cover, 153–54, 155, 156, 159, 162, 163–69
Tatum, Art, 63
technological change, cultural impacts of, xviii–xix, 151–52
television, 105, 108
Terhune, Albert Payson, 121
thermodynamics, second law of, 147–49
Thurber, James, 121
Time-Life Books, 142
Time/Warner, 22–23
Toklas, Alice B., 101
Tolstoy, Lev, 52
topical anthologies, 139–40
To the Finland Station (Wilson), 64, 72
Trilling, Lionel, 112, 126
Turgenev, Ivan, 52
Twain, Mark, 101, 131

Ulysses (Joyce), 10, 46

Index

Union of Soviet Socialist Republics
(USSR):
American Cold War views of,
112, 113, 118, 122–23
collapse of, 76, 77
samizdat writers in, 173, 174
unsolicited manuscripts, 43–44
Updike, John, 119–20
urbanism, suburban migration
from, 102, 105

Vonnegut, Kurt, xv, 189
Viacom, 11
Vietnam War, 62, 77, 112, 113, 118,
122, 124, 132
Viking Press, 11, 18, 89–90, 100
Villard mansion, 5, 7

Waldenbooks, 104
Wallace, Mike, 97, 99
Warhol, Andy, 6
Warner, Susan, 99
Washington, Bushrod, 169, 170
Washington, George, 169–70
Weber, Max, 52
Weems, Mason Locke, 169–71
West, Nathanael, 46
West Africa, CIA investigations in,
122
Whitman, Walt, 35, 52, 173

Whyte, W. H., 62
Wide, Wide World, The (Warner), 99
Wiener, Norbert, 143–47, 148–52
Wilbur, Richard, 119
Wilde, Oscar, 54, 55
Wilentz, Eli, 52–53, 63–64, 65
Wilentz, Ted, 52–53, 63–64, 65
Williams, Robin, 21
Wilson, Edmund, 52, 64, 72–74,
78, 119
American literature series con-
ceived by, 126–32, 133, 134,
136–38, 141
censorship difficulties of,
73–74
death of, 132
Wilson, Elena, 73
Wilson, Helen, 73
Windsor, Kathleen, 101
World Wide Web, 171–75
see also digital electronic publi-
cation; Internet
written language, xviii–xix
W. W. Norton & Company, 18, 94

Yahoo, publisher consortium on,
xiv–xv, xvi
Yeats, William Butler, 10, 52

Zuckerman, Mort, 155–57

Index

guilt, 92
impotence, 30
intercourse, 43
repression, 18, 57
sexuality, perverse, 19
'shaming' methods, 62
shock treatment, 134–6, 138–40
Simon, Hermann, 154n
sinequan, 142
social
  breakdown, 9, 187
  class, psychosis and, 60, 67
  crisis, 62–3
  environment, therapy, and, 9, 131–2
  isolation, 177, 187
  organization changes, 142
  rejection, 11, 187
  therapy, 9–10, 143, 147, 149–51, 154, 156–7, 161–3, 166
societies, differing, 51–5, 63–7, 87, 100, 185–6
Society for Autistic Children, 47n
society's attitude to mental illness, 9–12, 54, 67, 133, 145–7, 168–9
sociology, 161
speech,
  disturbed, 21, 33, 45, 91
  mania, in, 33
split mind, 35
Stanton, A.H., 158, 160
statistics, 8, 67–8, 79–80, 146–8, 152, 178
stelazine, 141
stupidity, apparent, 30
stupor, 31, 44, 118
subnormality, 59
suicide,
  affective psychotics, of, 28, 30–1
  age and, 32, 173, 175, 180
  compulsory powers and, 144
  depression, due to, 108–9, 138–9, 140
  differing societies, in, 186
  guilt reaction, as, 75, 103
  hallucinations, due to, 43

homicide rate and, 186
schizophrenia, in, 43–4, 135–6
sex ratio of, 175
statistics of, 79–80
symbol formation, 107
syphilis, 49

Takala, 53
Tchambuli, 52
Terman, L.M., 61
thiopentone, 134
thioridazine, 141
thought,
  abstract, 37–9, 44
  blocking, 39, 91
  disorder, 36–7, 39, 43–4, 119, 168
thymo-leptics, 136
tofranil, 136, 138
tranquillizers, 136, 139–40, 142, 181
transference, 76
tranylcypromine, 136
tremors, 18
trifluoperazine, 141
Trobriand islanders, 64
Trotter, Wilfrid, 162
tryptizol, 138
tyramine, 137

unconscious mind, 22, 24, 101–2
U.S.A., 7, 56, 145, 186–7

voices, hearing, 38, 42–3, 45

war, 160–1, 186
will, disorders of, 36, 41
Winnicott, Dr, 107
witchcraft, 151
withdrawal, 22, 31, 35, 44, 90–1, 118
Woolf, Leonard, 27
Woolf, Virginia, 27–8
Worthing experiment, 150

Young, Kimball, 53
Yurok, 53, 56

Zulus, 10–11
Zuni, 52

BIBLIOGRAPHY

Chandler, David, 'Postcards from the Edge', Introduction to Mark Power, *The Shipping Forecast*, Zelda Cheatle Press, 1996

Connelly, Charlie, *Attention All Shipping*, Abacus, 2004

Hodgson, Caroline, *For the Love of Radio 4*, Summersdale, 2014

Jefferson, Peter, *And Now the Shipping Forecast*, UIT Cambridge, 2011

Saunders, Geoff, *Report from Coastal Stations*, Suffix, 2011

THANK YOU

This book couldn't have been written without the co-operation of the BBC and the Met Office. In particular, I'd like to thank Chris Aldridge, senior presenter at the BBC, for his enthusiasm and for letting me sit in on his 00:48 reading. I am in awe of his consummate professionalism. There was a fantastic response from other announcers, past and present, too. Special thanks to: Carolyn Brown, Catriona Chase, Kathy Clugston, Andrew Crawford, Charlotte Green, Zeb Soanes – and Diana Speed for the tea! Many thanks too to Emma Sharples and Helen Chivers at the Met Office for supplying the data for the sea areas and for answering all my niggly questions. Last but not least, thanks to my editor Kate Fox at BBC Books for being a steady hand at the helm.

THE SHIPPING FORECAST

The Experience of Motherhood

Unknown girl in the maternity ward

Child, the current of your breath is six days long.
You lie, a small knuckle on my white bed;
lie, fisted like a snail, so small and strong
at my breast. Your lips are animals; you are fed
with love. At first hunger is not wrong.
The nurses nod their caps; you are shepherded
down starch halls with the other unnested throng
in wheeling baskets. You tip like a cup; your head
moving to my touch. You sense the way we belong.
But this is an institution bed.
You will not know me very long.

The doctors are enamel. They want to know
the facts. They guess about the man who left me,
some pendulum soul, going the way men go
and leave you full of child. But our case history
stays blank. All I did was let you grow.
Now we are here for all the ward to see
They thought I was strange, although
I never spoke a word. I burst empty
of you, letting you learn how the air is so.
The doctors chart the riddle they ask of me
and I turn my head away. I do not know.

Yours is the only face I recognise.
Bone at my bone, you drink my answers in.
Six times a day I prize
your need, the animals of your lips, your skin
growing warm and plump. I see your eyes
lifting their tents. They are blue stones, they begin
to outgrow their moss. You blink in surprise
and I wonder what you can see, my funny kin,
as you trouble my silence. I am a shelter of lies.
Should I learn to speak again, or hopeless in
such sanity will I touch some face I recognise?

The Millstone

Down the hall the baskets start back. My arms
fit you like a sleeve, they hold
catkins of your willows, and wild bee farms
of your nerves, each muscle and fold
of your first days. Your old man's face disarms
the nurses. But the doctors return to scold
me. I speak. It is you my silence harms.
I should have known; I should have told
them something to write down. My voice alarms
my throat. 'Name of father—none.' I hold
you and name you bastard in my arms.

And now that's that. There is nothing more
that I can say or lose.
Others have traded life before
and could not speak. I tighten to refuse
your owling eyes, my fragile visitor.
I touch your cheeks, like flowers. You bruise
against me. We unlearn. I am a shore
rocking you off. You break from me. I choose
your only way, my small inheritor
and hand you off, trembling the selves we lose.
Go child, who is my sin and nothing more.

ANNE SEXTON (born 1928)

(5) $4x^6 - 24x^5 + 57x^4 - 73x^3 + 57x^2 - 24x + 4 = 0$

$4x^3 - 24x^2 + 57x - 73 + \dfrac{57}{x} - \dfrac{24}{x^2} + \dfrac{4}{x^3} = 0$, by dividing by x^3;

$4\left(x^3 + \dfrac{1}{x^3}\right) - 24\left(x^2 + \dfrac{1}{x^2}\right) + 57\left(x + \dfrac{1}{x}\right) = 73$.

Let $x + \dfrac{1}{x} = z$; then, $x^2 + \dfrac{1}{x^2} = z^2 - 2$, and $x^3 + \dfrac{1}{x^3} = z^3 - 3z$

Therefore, $4(z^3 - 3z) - 24(z^2 - 2) + 57z = 73$,

$z^3 - 6z^2 + \dfrac{45}{4}z = \dfrac{25}{4}$.

To solve this equation by Cardan's Rule, Art. 441,
let $z = y + 2$; then, $y^3 - \dfrac{3}{4}y + \dfrac{1}{4} = 0$,

$y = \sqrt[3]{\left(-\dfrac{1}{8} + \sqrt{\dfrac{1}{64} - \dfrac{1}{64}}\right)} + \sqrt[3]{\left(-\dfrac{1}{8} - \sqrt{\dfrac{1}{64} - \dfrac{1}{64}}\right)}$
$= -\dfrac{1}{2} - \dfrac{1}{2} = -1$.

Dividing $y^3 - \dfrac{3}{4}y + \dfrac{1}{4}$ by $y + 1$, the quotient is $y^2 - y + \dfrac{1}{4}$;
therefore, $y^2 - y + \dfrac{1}{4} = 0$, and $y = +\dfrac{1}{2}$, and $+\dfrac{1}{2}$.

Therefore, $z = y + 2 = -1 + 2 = 1$, or $\dfrac{1}{2} + 2 = \dfrac{5}{2}$, and $\dfrac{5}{2}$.

Therefore, $x + \dfrac{1}{x} = 1$; whence, $x = \dfrac{1 \pm \sqrt{-3}}{2}$;

or $x + \dfrac{1}{x} = \dfrac{5}{2}$; whence, $x = 2$, or $\dfrac{1}{2}$.

Therefore, the six roots are $2, \dfrac{1}{2}, 2, \dfrac{1}{2}, \dfrac{1 + \sqrt{-3}}{2}$

and $\dfrac{1 - \sqrt{-3}}{2}$.

Article 444.

BINOMIAL EQUATIONS.

(1) Let $x^4 = 1$, then, $x^4 - 1 = 0$, and $(x^2 - 1)(x^2 + 1) = 0$.
$\therefore x^2 - 1 = 0$; whence, $x^2 = 1$, and $x = +1$ or -1.
Also, $x^2 + 1 = 0$; whence, $x^2 = -1$, and $x = +\sqrt{-1}$,
or, $-\sqrt{-1}$.

(2) Let $x^5 = 1$; then, $x^5 - 1 = 0$, and the equation is divisible by $x - 1$; $\therefore x - 1 = 0$, and $x = +1$.
Dividing $x^5 - 1$ by $x - 1$, and placing the quotient equal to zero, we have

$x^4 + x^3 + x^2 + x + 1 = 0$;

$x^2 + x + 1 + \dfrac{1}{x} + \dfrac{1}{x^2} = 0$, by dividing by x^2,

$x^2 + \dfrac{1}{x^2} + x + \dfrac{1}{x} = -1$.

Let $x+\dfrac{1}{x}=z$; then, $x^2+\dfrac{1}{x^2}=z^2-2$, and

$z^2+z=1$; whence, $z=\dfrac{-1\pm\sqrt{5}}{2}=a$.

$\therefore x+\dfrac{1}{x}=a$; whence, $x=\dfrac{a}{2}+\tfrac{1}{2}\sqrt{a^2-4}$, or $\dfrac{a}{2}-\tfrac{1}{2}\sqrt{a^2-4}$

and since a has two values, x will have four values.

$a^2=\dfrac{(-1\pm\sqrt{5})^2}{4}=\dfrac{6-2\sqrt{5}}{4}$, or $\dfrac{6+2\sqrt{5}}{4}$.

$x=\dfrac{a}{2}+\tfrac{1}{2}\sqrt{a^2-4}=\dfrac{-1+\sqrt{5}}{4}+\tfrac{1}{4}\sqrt{-10-2\sqrt{5}}$

$=\tfrac{1}{4}\{\sqrt{5}-1+\sqrt{(-10-2\sqrt{5})}\}$;

$x=\dfrac{a}{2}-\tfrac{1}{2}\sqrt{a^2-4}=\dfrac{-1+\sqrt{5}}{4}-\tfrac{1}{4}\sqrt{-10-2\sqrt{5}}$

$=\tfrac{1}{4}\{\sqrt{5}-1-\sqrt{(-10-2\sqrt{5})}\}$;

$x=-\dfrac{a}{2}+\tfrac{1}{2}\sqrt{a^2-4}=\dfrac{-1-\sqrt{5}}{4}+\tfrac{1}{4}\sqrt{-10+2\sqrt{5}}$

$=-\tfrac{1}{4}\{\sqrt{5}+1-\sqrt{(-10+2\sqrt{5})}\}$;

$x=\dfrac{a}{2}-\tfrac{1}{2}\sqrt{a^2-4}=\dfrac{-1-\sqrt{5}}{4}-\tfrac{1}{4}\sqrt{-10+2\sqrt{5}}$

$=-\tfrac{1}{4}\{\sqrt{5}+1+\sqrt{(-10+2\sqrt{5})}\}$.

INDEX

Gradually varied flow, 115, 118, 121
Greece, 27–30
Greek mill, 32
Ground water, 96, 182, 188–91

Hammurabi, 25
Harappa, 27
Head loss, 91, 103
Helmholtz, 49
Herodotus, 23, 24
Herschel, Clemens, 49
Hydraulic gradient, 100–1, 104
Hydraulic jump, 115, 118–19, 125
Hydraulic laboratory, 167
Hydraulic model, 49, 153–68
Hydraulics, 46, 50, 170
Hydrodynamics, 52
Hydrograph, 139, 140
Hydrologic cycle, 170–72
Hydrologic Decade, 192, 216
Hydrology, 169–92
Hydrostatics, 52–69

Ideal fluid, 45
Impulse–momentum equation, 93–4
Indus River, 27
Infiltration, 179–80, 182–3
Interception, 179
Interflow, 182
Irrigation engineering, 208–11

Joseph's Well, 26

Kelvin, Lord, 49
Kepler, Johannes, 37
Knossos, 27

Lagrange, Joseph, 44–5, 74
Lamb, Sir Horace, 49
Laminar flow, 49, 70–71, 117–18
Laplace, Pierre, 45
Leonardo da Vinci, 35, 47, 128

Manning formula, 123
Mariotte, Edme, 38
Medium theory, 29, 35, 40
Metacentre, 68
Models, hydraulic, 49, 95, 153–68
Mohenjo-daro, 27
Momentum equation, 85, 93–4
Motion, laws of, 39

Newton, Sir Isaac, 29, 39–40, 45, 65
Nile River, 22
Nineveh, 26
Non uniform flow, 81, 115–18
Norse mill, 32

Orifice flow, 38, 91–2, 98
Orifice meter, 93

Pascal, Blaise, 38
Pelton wheel, 94, 95, 151
Pendulation, 110
Percolation, 24, 96, 157, 161, 191
Persia, 34
Philoponus, Ionnes, 29, 35
Phoenicians, 27, 28
Pipe: branching, 105
  flow in a, 99–113
  'friction', 103–4
  material, 31, 111
  network, 106
  strength, 110
Plato, 28, 193
Pollution, 206–7, 218
Prandtl, Ludwig, 50
Precipitation, 171, 173–9
Pressure: absolute, 56
  atmospheric, 56
  bursting, 101
  gauge, 56
  intensity of, 55, 57–9
Pressure wave, 107–9
Project investigation, 161–2
Pump: air-lift, 149–50
  axial-flow, 147
  centrifugal, 36, 144–7
  multi-stage, 146
  piston, 148
  radial, 147
  rotary, 149
Pumps, 142–50

Rainfall, 173–9
Rapidly varied flow, 118–19
Rawlinson, Sir Robert, 204
Recharge, 190
Research, 49–50
Resistance coefficient, 103
Reynolds, Osborne, 49, 77, 165
Reynolds number, 77, 164, 165, 166
Ripples, 129–30
River engineering, 114–26, 211–14

INDEX

Rome, 30–34
Rotating cup, 65–6
Roughness, 73, 103
Rouse, Hunter, 49, 137
Run-off, 178, 182, 184–5
Russell, John Scott, 138, 165

Sailing ships, 27
Samos, 30
Seiche, 131
Sewerage system, 204–8
Sherman, L. K., 185
Ship stability, 67–8
Similarity, 162–3
Siphon, 23, 104
Skin friction, 76
Smeaton, John, 47
Specific speed, 147
Spray irrigation, 210–11, 219
Steady flow, 81, 86
Stevin, Simon, 37
Storm intensity, 177–8
Stream function, 44
Streamline, 44, 95
Streamlining, 76
Sub-critical flow, 119–22, 124
Submerged bodies, 68
Suez Canal, 24
Super-critical flow, 119–22, 124
Surface tension, 129
Surge, 109, 138
Surge tank, 109–10

Thales of Miletus, 28
Three-reservoir problem, 105
Tidal wave, 131
Tigris River, 25
Torricelli, Evangelista, 36, 38, 91–2
Transpiration, 180–81
Transposition of storms, 179
Tsunami, 131
Turbines, 94, 95, 150–52
Turbulent flow, 49, 71, 117–18

Uniform flow, 81
Unit hydrograph, 185
United Nations, 216
Unsteady flow, 86, 106–10
Uplift pressure, 63

Vapour, 84, 143, 173
Velocity distribution, 83
Venturi meter, 93
Viscosity, 40, 49, 70–79, 143
Viscous drag, 53
Vitruvius, 32

Waste-water disposal, 204–8
Water-hammer, 106–10, 143
Water consumption, 13–15
Water resources planning, 214–15
Water supply engineering, 102, 198–203
Water table, 182
Water wheel, 32, 34, 46, 47, 150
Wave: celerity, 120, 130, 132, 133, 138
 length, 130, 131
 motion, 127–41, 164
 reflection, 136
 refraction, 135
 train, 132
Waves: breaking, 134
 capillary, 129–30
 deep water, 128
 flood, 139–40
 gravity, 130–38
 interfacial, 140–41
 oscillatory, 127–38
 shallow water 133
 solitary, 137–8
Wells, 96, 189–90
Wheel, 10

Yield, 187

Index

Tuckett, Dr Reginald, 15–16, 33, 111, 140, 176–7

Uganda for a Holiday (Treves), 168
University College Hospital, London, 41
University of Strasbourg, 145

Valentine, Rev. Tristram, 153–4
Vaughan, Dr Charles John, 106
Veronese, Paolo, 137
Victoria, Queen, 52, 126, 166–7; Diamond Jubilee of, 166, 174–5
Viski, Dr Károly, 142
von Recklinghausen, *see* Recklinghausen, Frederick Daniel von

Wadman, Tilly, 135
Walpole, Sir Robert, 154
Watts, Isaac, 91
Weaker Sex, The (Pinero), 133
Weber, Dr F. Parkes, 147–8
Wellesley, the Hon. Mrs Gerald, 187, 189
Wellington, duke of, 132
Weston, George, 72
Whitechapel, London, 14, 39, 138
Whitechapel Road, 14, 16; freak-shop in, 11–12, 15–16, 17–20, 23, 33, 40, 43, 88, 89, 90, 140, 186, 190–91, 193–4
Whittington, Salop., 175
Wilberforce, Samuel, bishop of Winchester, 132
Wilson, S. A. Kinnier, 151
Wimpole Street, Treves's house and practice in, 33, 164; Elephant Man's visit to, 125–6, 206
Wirksworth, Derbyshire, 31
Wombwell, George, 51–2, 53
Wombwell's Royal Menagerie, 51–5
Wood, Mrs John, 77
World's Fair, 174

Yakovac, Dr William, 57
Young & Sandy, 77

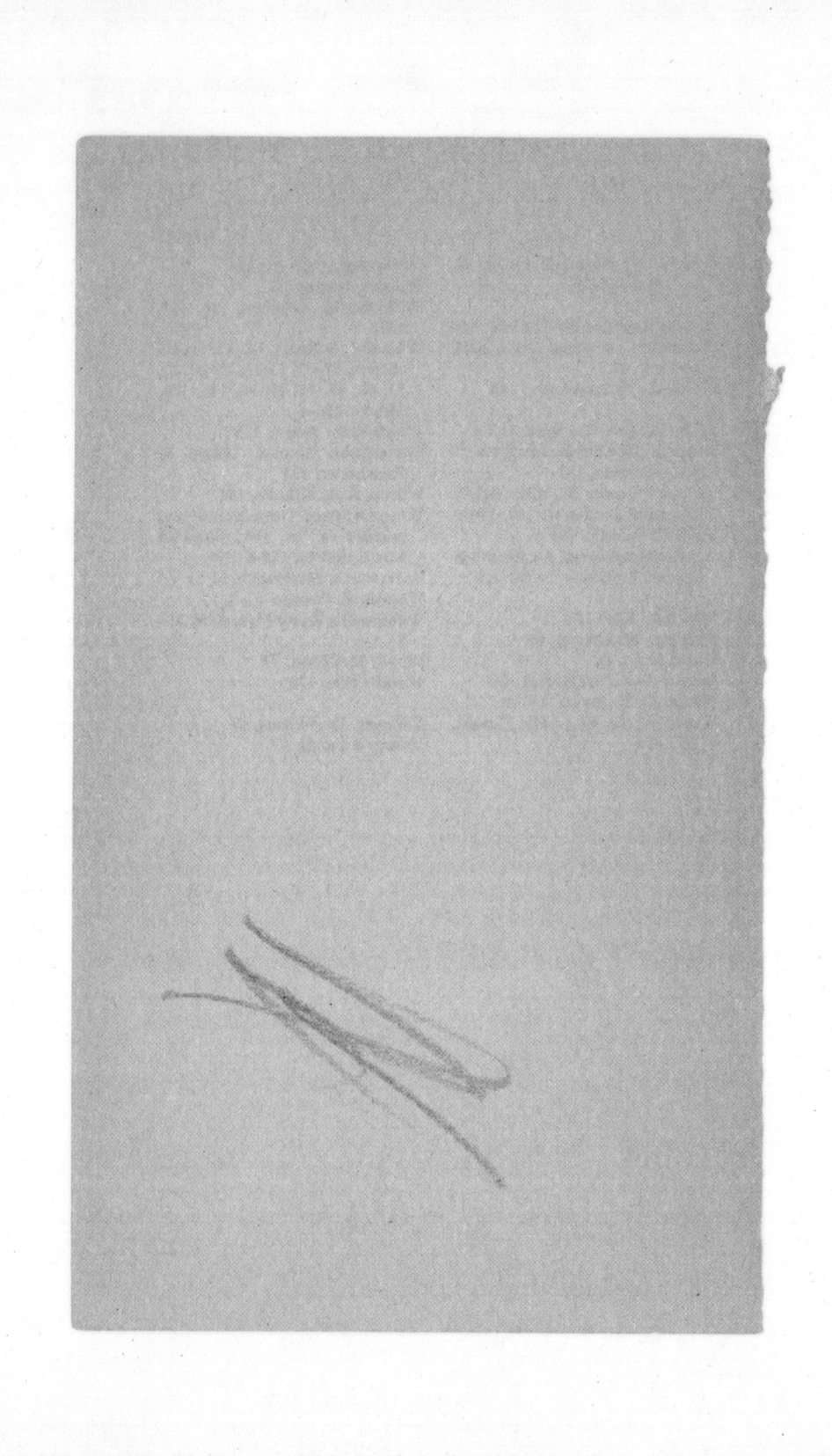

company and affection he perpetually longed. Not that there was here any inherent defect, or that he was unable to recognise or rejoice in the beauty of the world. But, just as one of the greatest of all scholars was never known to allude to the Alps except as a natural obstacle, or George Howard Wilkinson's friends used to amuse themselves " with trying to teach him how to look on a sunset as a sunset," so was Dick the victim, deliberate and unashamed, of the " single eye." If you did not know that Robert Browning wrote *Parting at Morning*, you might with fair reason have ascribed it to Dick Sheppard:

Round the cape of a sudden came the sea,
    And the sun looked over the mountain's rim;
And straight was a path of gold for him,
    And the need of a world of men for me.

Something he had which he shared with all the saints, but to no one of them could you liken him. That is one of the reasons why he will never be forgotten by his friends.

Douglas, Bill 38
Doyle, Sir Arthur Conan 29
Dunne, Irene 23
Durgnat, Raymond 187, 188, 190
Eidsvik, Charles 118
Eilenberg, Susan 108
Emerson, Ralph Waldo 28, 29, 31
Falk, Peter 126
Fassbinder, Rainer Werner 46
Field, Betty 39
Fields, W C 117
Fischer, Michael 19, 24
Fleishman, Avrom 74, 86
Fonda, Henry 40
Forman, Miloš 2, 103
Freud, Sigmund 186
Fried, Michael 55, 56
Garbo, Greta 16, 17, 22, 96, 104, 121, 125
Grande illusion, La (Grand Illusion) 22
Grant, Cary 23
Greuze, Jean Baptiste 55
Hawks, Howard 193
Heidegger, Martin 29, 53, 55, 179
Hitchcock, Alfred 13, 14, 19, 40, 41, 176, 181, 182, 184
Hodsdon, Barrett 64
Hollywood 42, 43, 57, 58, 60, 63, 95, 193
Horton, Andrew 115, 117
Husserl, Edmund Gustav Albrecht 197
It Happened One Night 140
James, Henry 20
Jeanne Dielman, 23 Quai du Commerce, 1080 Bruxelles 207
Johnson, Dots M 43
Journal d'un curé de campagne (Diary of a Country Priest) 1, 2, 50, 71, 79, 87-89, 94-99, 103, 104, 122, 208, 209, 211
Kant, Immanuel 195
Keane, Marian 21
Keaton, Buster 49, 117
Kes 41-43
Kierkegaard, Søren 28
King Lear 12
Kulešov, Lev 73
Lásky jedné plavovlásky (A Blonde in Love/Loves of a Blonde) 2, 4, 50, 103, 104, 115-118, 121-123, 125-132, 139, 186, 208, 209, 212
Late Spring see *Banshun*
Laurel and Hardy 25, 26, 116, 117
Laydu, Claude 71, 73, 95, 96, 98
Leitch, Thomas M 15, 16
Loach, Ken 41, 42
Loves of a Blonde see *Lásky jedné plavovlásky*
McCarey, Leo 23
Marcus, Millicent 48, 49
Margulies, Ivone 207
Martin, Adrian 64
Marx Brothers 117, 193, 194
Masao, Mishima 136
Matisse, Henri 174
"melkmeisje, Het" ("Woman Pouring Milk") 53-57
Milne, Tom 174, 175
Modigliani, Amedeo 174
Morte a Venezia (Death in Venice) 46
Mr. Smith Goes to Washington 95-99, 103, 206, 215
Mulhall, Stephen 17-19, 25, 104
Music Box, The 117
My Childhood 38, 48
neo-realism 45
Noh drama 150, 152-156, 158, 213
Novak, Kim 13, 14
Ophüls, Max 59, 63, 151
Othello 13
Ozu, Yasujirō 2, 46, 57
Paisà (Paisan) 43, 45
Pather Panchali 36, 38

Perkins, V F
   2, 14, 19, 20, 30, 59-63
Phillips, Adam
   64, 107, 108, 186-189
Philosophical Investigations
   29, 179
Poe, Edgar Allan   29, 61, 179
Psychopathology of Everyday Life, The   186
Pucholt, Vladimír   109
"Purloined Letter, The"
   29, 61, 179
Quester, Hugues   175
Rains, Claude   98
Ray, Nicholas   63
Ray, Satyajit   36
Reformation   18
Règle du jeu, La (The Rules of the Game)   22
Renoir, Jean   22, 39, 159
Resnais, Alain   184
Rivette, Jacques   46
Rohmer, Eric
   2, 170, 176, 187, 193
Rossellini, Roberto   43, 45
Rothman, William   21
Rowlands, Gena   126
Rules of the Game, The see La Règle du jeu
Ruth, Babe (George Herman)   3
Schumann, Robert   175, 192
Scott, Zachary   39
Setsuko, Hara   135
Shakespeare, William   12
Sirk, Douglas   63, 161
Snow, Edward   53-55
Socialism   4, 122

Southerner, The   39
"Spring" Sonata (Beethoven)   170
Staiger, Janet   57, 58
Stanwyck, Barbara   161
Stewart, James   13, 14, 20, 95-98
Strangers on a Train
   181, 183-185, 187, 201, 207, 215
Tale of Springtime, A see Conte de printemps
Tarkovskij, Andrej   46
Teyssèdre, Anne   172
Thompson, Kristin   57, 58
Thoreau, Henry David   24
Three Stooges, The   117
To Have and Have Not   193
Umberto D
   36, 46, 47, 53, 56, 59, 61, 209
Vermeer, Jan   53-57
Vertigo
   13-16, 19-22, 24, 206, 214
Visconti, Luchino   46
Walker, Michael   163
Welles, Orson   159
Wilson, George M   2, 49, 58-62
Wittgenstein, Ludwig
   24, 29, 53, 61, 179
"Woman Pouring Milk" see "Het melkmeisje"
Woman Under the Influence, A
   126-132, 206, 215
World Viewed, The   18, 87
Wrong Man, The   40
Wyler, William   159
Zavattini, Cesare   49
Zéro de Conduite (Zero for Conduct)   22

Thanks:

Graeme Macrae Burnet, I thank you for every single walk, trip and thought, I wouldn't have been able to write this book without your wisdom, generosity and kindness.

Goethe-Institut Glasgow, thank you so much for your fantastic and uncomplicated help.

The Hielan Jessie and, of course, Tom (I wish I knew your surname).

A big shout out goes to Rachel Ward, my gifted translator, and to absolutely everyone at Orenda Books, especially Karen Sullivan, who I adore.

Translator acknowledgements:
Thank you to all the GI Glasgow Stammtischlers for your help, and especially Jackie Bornfleth and Isabel Stainsby.

if the Boy had never existed at all. He had existed and would always exist. She had a sudden conviction that she carried life – and she thought proudly: Let them get over that if they can; let them get over that. She turned out on to the front opposite the Palace Pier and began to walk firmly away from the direction of her home towards Frank's. There was something to be salvaged from that house and room, something else they wouldn't be able to get over – his voice speaking a message to her: if there was a child, speaking to the child. "If he loved you," the priest had said, "that shows . . ." She walked rapidly in the thin June sunlight towards the worst horror of all.

(Alfred A. Knopf, 2015). Compilation copyright © 2015 by Marge Piercy. Used by permission of Alfred A. Knopf, an imprint of the Knopf Doubleday Publishing Group, a division of Penguin Random House LLC. All rights reserved.

Pierpoint, Katherine: 'Cats Are Otherwise' from *Truffle Beds* (Faber, 1995). Reprinted by permission of Faber & Faber Ltd. © Katherine Pierpoint, 1995.

Plath, Sylvia: 'Mushrooms' from *Collected Poems*, ed. Ted Hughes (Faber, 1981). Reprinted by permission of Faber & Faber Ltd. © Sylvia Plath, 1981.

Reid, Christopher: 'Cycle' from *Selected Poems* (Faber, 2011). Reprinted by permission of Rogers, Coleridge & White © Christopher Reid, 2011.

Riley, Denise: 'Tree seen from bed' from *Say Something Back* (Picador, 2016) © Denise Riley, 2016.

Riordan, Maurice: 'The Red Sea' from *The Holy Land* (Faber, 2007). Reprinted by permission of Faber & Faber Ltd. © Maurice Riordan, 2007.

Rossetti, Dante Gabriel: 'The Woodspurge'. This work is in the public domain.

Shakespeare, William 52: 'Sonnet 104' ('To me, fair friend'). This work is in the public domain.

Simic, Charles: 'Fork' from *Charles Simic: Selected Early Poems* (George Braziller Inc., 1999) Copyright © 1999 by Charles Simic. Reprinted with the permission of George Braziller, Inc. (New York), www.georgebraziller.com. All rights reserved.

Sprackland, Jean: 'A Phone off the Hook' from *Tilt* (Jonathan Cape, 2007) Reprinted by permission of The Random House Group Limited. © Jean Sprackland 2007.

Strand, Mark: 'Pot Roast' from *The New Yorker* (Conde Nast, 1977). Reprinted by permission of Conde Nast © Mark Strand, 1977.

Thomas, Edward: 'Adlestrop' from Selected Poems, ed. Matthew Hollis (Faber & Faber, 2011)

Walcott, Derek: 'Adieu foulard...' (Chapter X from 'Tales of the Islands') Selected Poems, ed. Edward Baugh (Faber, 2007). Reprinted by permission of Faber & Faber Ltd. © Derek Walcott, 2007.

Wetherald, Ethelwyn: 'The Fields of Dark'. This work is in the public domain.

Wordsworth, Dorothy: 'Floating Island'. This work is in the public domain.

Wordsworth, William: 'The Solitary Reaper' and 'Composed upon Westminster Bridge'. These works are in the public domain.

Wright, James: 'A Blessing' from *Above the River: The Complete Poems and Selected Prose*. Reprinted by permission of Wesleyan University Press © James Wright, 1990.

Yeats, W. B.: 'The Lake Isle of Innisfree'. This work is in the public domain.

Yeh, Jane: 'Walrus' from *The Ninjas* (Carcanet, 2012) Reprinted by permission of Carcanet © Jane Yeh, 2012.

Young, Andrew: 'Field-Glasses' from *Selected Poems* (Carcanet, 1998) Reprinted by permission of Carcanet © Andrew Young 1998.

Young, Kevin: 'I shall be released' from *Dear Darkness Poems* (Knopf, 2008). Reprinted by permission of Alfred A. Knopf, an imprint of the Knopf Doubleday Publishing Group, a division of Penguin Random House LLC. All rights reserved. Copyright © Kevin Young, 2008.

Every effort has been made to contact copyright holders for permission to reproduce the material in this book. In the case of any inadvertent oversight, the publishers will include an appropriate acknowledgement in future editions.

explain that one? Watch playing up, was it?"

"Clare did warn me but I went in straightaway on the basis that it could've saved Kerry's life or prevented serious injury to her."

"Ah, I see," John retorted showily. "You had reason to believe she was in the house, then?"

Brett glanced out of the window and took a deep breath.

Before he could answer, John said, "I'll take that as a yes." Smiling at Brett and tossing the papers back at him, he added, "So, put it in the report and it's all done." His tone fell neatly between annoyance and endorsement.

"Thank you, sir," Brett replied. "And Louise? You're recommending…?"

John grimaced at the telephone as its ringing interrupted them. "Hang on, you two," he ordered as he picked up the receiver. Answering the call brusquely, he barked, "Macfarlane". He drummed his fingers on his desk, listened for a few seconds and then muttered, "A fire. What's it got to do with me? Hasn't the fire brigade squirted water on it?" John's fingers froze. "I see. Unpleasant. Very unpleasant. Where is it?" After noting the reply, John looked at Brett and Clare across the desk as he announced into the telephone, "Yeah, I've got someone here who'll take it on. The perfect team."

Latin America

Beyond the Border: A New Age in Latin American Women's Fiction edited by Nora Erro-Peralta and Caridad Silva-Núñez.
ISBN: 0-939416-42-5 24.95 cloth;
ISBN: 0-939416-43-3 12.95 paper.

The Little School: Tales of Disappearance and Survival in Argentina by Alicia Partnoy.
ISBN: 0-939416-08-5 21.95 cloth;
ISBN: 0-939416-07-7 9.95 paper.

Revenge of the Apple by Alicia Partnoy.
ISBN: 0-939416-62-X 24.95 cloth;
ISBN: 0-939416-63-8 8.95 paper.

You Can't Drown the Fire: Latin American Women Writing in Exile edited by Alicia Partnoy.
ISBN: 0-939416-16-6 24.95 cloth;
ISBN: 0-939416-17-4 9.95 paper.

Autobiography, Biography, Letters

Peggy Deery: An Irish Family at War by Nell McCafferty.
ISBN: 0-939416-38-7 24.95 cloth;
ISBN: 0-939416-39-5 9.95 paper.

The Shape of Red: Insider/Outsider Reflections by Ruth Hubbard and Margaret Randall.
ISBN: 0-939416-19-0 24.95 cloth;
ISBN: 0-939416-18-2 9.95 paper.

Women & Honor: Some Notes on Lying by Adrienne Rich.
ISBN: 0-939416-44-1 3.95 paper.

Animal Rights

And a Deer's Ear, Eagle's Song and Bear's Grace: Relationships Between Animals and Women edited by Theresa Corrigan and Stephanie T. Hoppe.
ISBN: 0-939416-38-7 24.95 cloth;
ISBN: 0-939416-39-5 9.95 paper.

With a Fly's Eye, Whale's Wit and Woman's Heart: Relationships Between Animals and Women edited by Theresa Corrigan and Stephanie T. Hoppe.
ISBN: 0-939416-24-7 24.95 cloth;
ISBN: 0-939416-25-5 9.95 paper.

Ordering Books

Since 1980, Cleis Press has published progressive books by women. We welcome your order and will ship your books as quickly as possible. Individual orders must be prepaid (U.S. dollars only). Please add 15% shipping. Pennsylvania residents add 6% sales tax. Mail orders to Cleis Press, P.O. Box 8933, Pittsburgh, Pennsylvania 15221. MasterCard and Visa orders: include account number, expiration date, and signature. Fax your credit card order to (412) 937-1567. Or, telephone us Monday through Friday, 9 am–5 pm EST at (412) 937-1555.

met, her needs grew, and the kiss went on, deepening as Jake's hunger matched her own.

Pulling back, Kara murmured into his neck. "Mmm, I really should take that bath. I'm pretty grimy."

Gray-green eyes smiled into hers. "How about a shower? It's quicker." He stood, pulling her up with him. "I'll even wash your back."

"Maybe you could join me. It saves water. I've always been interested in water conservation, haven't you?"

Jake's grin widened as he led her toward the bathroom, already tugging off his shirt. "Not until today I haven't, but I think I'll become a strong advocate if it involves shared showers with you."

With his finger Jake traced the red mark along her neck left by the breaking off of her necklace. "I'll get your gold chain fixed for you tomorrow," he said, placing a soft kiss on the spot.

"Thank you."

His smile was filled with feeling. "That's when I knew you cared more than you thought you did, when you got so upset over breaking the chain I'd given you."

"I've never been without it since you put it on my neck. I don't think I realized what it came to represent. When it fell, I suddenly felt I'd broken the last link with you, that I'd lost you, too."

Jake moved her into his arms, his hands rubbing her back. "You will never, ever have to worry about losing me. I love you, Kara. I'm never going to let you go."

"I'm going to hold you to that," Kara said, raising her lips to kiss the man she loved, secure at last in the knowledge that she'd found the only home she'd ever need.

* * * * *

Silhouette Special Edition

COMING NEXT MONTH

THROUGH ALL ETERNITY
Sondra Stanford

Jeff Chappel was vital, dynamic — fiercely protective of those he loved. And he had his eye on Lila... How was she going to persuade the gentle giant that *protection* was not what she needed from him?

NEVER LET GO
Sherryl Woods

Hospital psychologist Mallory Blake had heard rumours that ace surgeon Justin Whitmore utterly lacked compassion. But when he reached out to one of her young patients, Mallory glimpsed the warmth beneath his frosty exterior. Why would such a caring man foster such a cold reputation?

SILENT PARTNER
Celeste Hamilton

Melissa Chambers needed capital to turn the mansion she'd inherited into Chattanooga's finest restaurant. Hunt Kirkland had the capital and wanted the perfect location. However, Melissa wanted a silent partner and there was no way he could agree to that. Was there room for compromise?

archway on the further side of the room they could see the bottom of the staircase that led up to the higher floors. Just under the crown of the arch dangled a pair of feet.

'Mr Savage!'

Slowly, very slowly, like two unhurried compass needles, the feet turned towards the right; north, north-east, east, south-east, south, south-south-west; then paused, and after a few seconds, turned as unhurriedly back towards the left. South-south-west, south, south-east, east . . .

TITLES BY ALDOUS HUXLEY
IN PAPERBACK FROM GRAFTON BOOKS

Crome Yellow
Antic Hay
Those Barren Leaves
Along the Road*
Jesting Pilate*
Point Counter Point
Brief Candles
Music at Night
Brave New World
Texts and Pretexts
Beyond the Mexique Bay*
Eyeless in Gaza
After Many a Summer
Grey Eminence
The Art of Seeing
Time Must Have a Stop
The Perennial Philosophy
Ape and Essence
The Gioconda Smile and Other Stories
The Devils of Loudun
The Doors of Perception/Heaven and Hell
The Genius and the Goddess
Brave New World Revisited
Island
The Human Situation

*PUBLISHED IN PALADIN

"I don't know what community character you're talking about. It's things like the Fourth of July parade and the fireworks that give our town character. I refuse to vote against the fireworks," declared Marzetti, who had grown hot around the collar.

"Well said," drawled Bud Collins.

"Is this a vote?" Howard White seemed uncharacteristically confused.

The others nodded.

"Two for and two against. I guess it's up to me."

The room was silent.

"My inclination is to hold the fireworks. It's been a tradition in this town for as long as I've been here and I hate to see it end." White sighed. "But I truly believe it would be irresponsible and futile to ignore the state regulation. It would set a bad precedent and it would cost us dearly in the end. It's with great sorrow that I vote to discontinue the fireworks display."

He had hardly finished speaking when Scratch Hallett was on his feet, marching out of the room. He paused at the door. "This isn't the end of this," he declared, as he set his VFW hat on hs head. "We may have lost the battle, but we haven't lost the war!"

BOOK YOUR PLACE ON OUR WEBSITE AND MAKE THE READING CONNECTION!

We've created a customized website just for our very special readers, where you can get the inside scoop on everything that's going on with Zebra, Pinnacle and Kensington books.

When you come online, you'll have the exciting opportunity to:

- View covers of upcoming books
- Read sample chapters
- Learn about our future publishing schedule (listed by publication month *and author*)
- Find out when your favorite authors will be visiting a city near you
- Search for and order backlist books from our online catalog
- Check out author bios and background information
- Send e-mail to your favorite authors
- Meet the Kensington staff online
- Join us in weekly chats with authors, readers and other guests
- Get writing guidelines
- AND MUCH MORE!

Visit our website at
http://www.kensingtonbooks.com

the company failed to tell them that Maxwell House coffee is addictive, and demanded compensation for the headaches and insomnia they suffered in prison.

8. Vicki Daily of Jackson, Wyoming filed a lawsuit in July 1993 against the widow of the man she had earlier run over and killed in her pick-up truck. Ms Daily demanded compensation from the widow for the "grave and crippling psychological injuries" she suffered while watching the 56-year-old man die.

9. In December 1993 a New York appeals court rejected housewife Edna Hobbs's lawsuit against a company that sold a time-saving kitchen device called The Clapper. The complainant said that in order to turn her appliances on, she clapped until her hands bled. The judge found that Mrs Hobbs had merely failed to adjust the sensitivity controls.

10. In 1994 a handicapped French woman, Yvette LeMons, sued the owner of her rented Toulouse flat for $25,000. Lawyers acting for Miss

LeMons said the apartment owner had allowed termites to enter the premises, which had then eaten her wooden leg, causing her to fall down and break her arm.

INDEX

Stratford, Boswell's visit to, 146
Stuart, James, 203
Suard, Jean Baptiste, and Sterne, 170-171
Sutton-in-the-Forest, Sterne's appointment to the living of, 144
Swift, Dean, and Sterne, 171

Taylor, Dr. John, Boswell's visit to, 63
Temple, Richard Grenville, Earl, and Wilkes, 204-205, 206, 210, 214, 220, 234, 235; and the King's speech, 208-209
Temple, Rev. William Johnson, 17, 18, 24, 70; Boswell's friendship with, 17, 24, 32, 39, 58; his letters to, on his drinking, 63; and on his Journal, 74-75
The Club, Gibbon a member of, 111, 116; Johnson at, 116
Thrale, Henry, 64
Thrale, Mrs. Hester, and Johnson, 45-46, 47, 48, 50-51, 64-65; her memoirs, 51; her marriage with Piozzi, 51, 64
Thrale, Queenie, and her mother's marriage, 64-65
Topham, Dr., his dispute with Dr. Fountayne, 156-157
Travis, George, 116

Utrecht, 29, 37

Vasseur, Thérèse le, 37
Vindication (Gibbon), 116
Voltaire, François Marie Arouet de, and Boswell, 32; and Gibbon, 91, 102; and Sterne, 170, 171; and Wilkes, 232

W——t, Miss, and Boswell, 17-18, 19
Walpole, Horace, 13, 35, 41, 99, 117, 119-120
Warburton, William, Bishop of Gloucester, and Sterne, 164; and the debate on the *Essay*, 220
West Wycombe Park and the Hell Fire Club, 202
Weymouth, Lord, and Wilkes, 238, 239
Whitehead, Paul, 204

Whitfield, George, and Wilkes, 242
Wilkes, John, his wit, 11, 219n., 235; character and characteristics, 12, 199, 200, 201, 205, 208, 222, 224, 228, 235, 239, 242-243; appearance, 13, 199, 201, 215, 237, 244; the cry of "Wilkes and Liberty," 42, 216, 243; and Boswell, 35, 75, 225, 227-228; and the City of London, 57, 234, 241; and Johnson, 73, 229-230; and Gibbon, 96, 97, 206; his ancestry, 200; homes and marriage, 200; and the Hell Fire Club, 204; elected Member for Aylesbury, 204-205; his financial position, 205, 233; posts applied for, 205; as journalist for the Opposition, 205-206; and the *North Briton* (q.v.), 206; his writing, style and quality of, 206, 208; his military service, 206; his duels, 207-208, 221-222; Pitt on, 209; and the advance copy of the King's speech, 209 *et seq.*; a patriot by accident, 210, 233; arrest and imprisonment of, 213-214; seizure of his private correspondence, 214, 216, 232; rousing of public sympathy 214-215; Hogarth's caricature of, 215; release of, and damages for wrongful arrest, 215-216; and general warrants, 216, 232, 242; motion against carried, 218-219; and his supporters, 220, 224; in Paris and Italy, 223, 225, 228 *et seq.*; and his autobiography, 225; and Churchill, 226-227; and Voltaire, 232; his return to England, 233; and the preservation of English liberties, 233, 243; his appeal to the King for pardon, 233; standing of, for Middlesex, 234, 235; his conception of liberty, 236; visit to Bath, 237; his legal position, 237; trial of, 237-238; and generosity of his supporters, 238-239, 242; expulsion of, from Parliament, and the result, 239-240; his release, 241; the issues he fought for, 241, 242; method of, with his opponents, 241; return of, to Parliament, 241; on Faith, Hope, and Charity, 243; influence of, on foreign events, 243-244; death of,

and his epitaph, 244; as an ancestor, 247, 248
Wilkes, Mrs. John, 200; her estate near Aylesbury, 201; separation of, from her husband, 201
Wilkes, Polly, her father's love for, 201, 207, 217, 224, 228, 234n., 244; letter to, on his duel, 222
Williams, Anna, 27, 49, 65, 69
Winckelman, Johann Joachim, and Sterne, 230

Worsley, Sir Thomas, 94, 97, 206

York and Albany, Frederick Augustus, Duke of, 21, 95, 164-165, 179
York, Bishop of, and Sterne, 187
York, Sterne's life in, 144-145

Zuylen, Isabella (Zélide) de, and Boswell, 30-31, 44

Bevis gathered the harebell, and ran with the flower in his hand down the hill, and as he ran the wild thyme kissed his feet and said "Come again, Bevis, come again." At the bottom of the hill the waggon was loaded now; so they lifted him up, and he rode home on the broad back of the leader.

DISTRIBUTORS
for Wordsworth Children's Classics

AUSTRALIA, BRUNEI & MALAYSIA

Reed Editions
22 Salmon Street
Port Melbourne
Vic 3207
Australia
Tel: (03) 646 6716
Fax: (03) 646 6925

GERMANY, AUSTRIA & SWITZERLAND

Swan Buch-Marketing GmbH
Goldscheuerstraße 16
D-7640 Kehl am Rhein
Germany

GREAT BRITAIN & IRELAND

Wordsworth Editions Ltd
Cumberland House
Crib Street
Ware
Hertfordshire SG12 9ET

INDIA

Om Book Service
1690 First Floor
Nai Sarak, Delhi - 110006
Tel: 3279823/3265303
Fax: 3278091

NEW ZEALAND

Whitcoulls Limited
Private Bag 92098, Auckland

SINGAPORE

Book Station
18 Leo Drive
Singapore
Tel: 4511998
Fax: 4529188

SOUTHERN AFRICA

Struik Book Distributors (Pty) Ltd
Graph Avenue
Montague Gardens
7441
P O Box 193
Maitland
7405
South Africa
Tel: (021) 551-5900
Fax: (021) 551-1124

USA, CANADA & MEXICO

Universal Sales & Marketing
230 Fifth Avenue
Suite 1212
New York, NY 10001 USA
Tel: 212-481-3500
Fax: 212-481-3534

ITALY

Magis Books
Piazza della Vittoria 1/C
42100 Reggio Emilia
Tel: 0522-452303
Fax: 0522-452845

yelled, 'Hey! He's cheating!' and went after him. Samson Two dived in underneath them. Next thing, they were pulling and shoving each other in front of the multifunctional displays.

And the next thing after that: a long screeching noise. Then a jolt, as though we'd been caught on a bungee. Then we spun round. And round. And round. And over and round. Fast. And random. Like the cage of the Cosmic.

And a light strobed off and on and off like blue lightning.

And somewhere in the middle of it the voice of Drax Control was shouting.

Then it stopped.

Then it shouted.

Then it stopped again.

The Earth vanished.

And then came back.

Then vanished.

And then came back.

And then we stopped rolling.

And Earth was gone.

No one said a word.

We drifted over to the window and pressed our faces against the glass, looking for some sign of it.

It was very quiet. And very dark. And very, very scary.

Frank Cottrell Boyce
Chitty Chitty BANG BANG
Flies Again

First it Coughs...

Soon it SPLutteRs...

Then it cHuGs...

Next it ROARS...

It's no ordinary car, it's a car with a mind of its own! This is a car that can

FLY!

Race into adventure with the first-ever sequel to Ian Fleming's *Chitty Chitty Bang Bang*

I suddenly felt very warmly towards my father – that's to say towards the one who had brought me up. I wished he was here, just back from the office, running through the day's freshest examples of parental spite: Gerda Loines and Marie Baddeley and Ilona Gayne. I couldn't summon up any such enthusiasm for Menashe, despite his stupendous memory for my mother's name. I've said that they have sentimental secrets in their lives, these arithmetical city businessmen with their silvered moustaches; but I was damned if Menashe's sentimental secret was going to be me.

I left Finchley almost as speedily as I'd left it on the day I very nearly found Asimova in my old wardrobe. I didn't bother looking in at Tooting. I knew exactly what I'd find there – Rabika Flatman taking unscrupulous advantage of my long-standing passion for her, and my father – utterly confounded by his family's clamour for individuation – distantly amused by something or other, and largely indifferent to Rabika and to me. That, I decided, was the quality I most liked in him. He had never bothered to get to know me and had never encouraged me to get to know him. He had not been icy, he simply had not been very interested in relationships. How tactful of him, if I wasn't his son, not to have attempted to make me think I was; how civilized of him not to have tried to make me *his*. No wonder I was fond of him.

So it wasn't necessary for me to see him again before I left. I knew what I wanted to know. It was best – just in case I was tempted into some last minute backsliding – to get away quickly. I didn't want to catch myself asking who or whose I was again, just for old times' sake. Not in Finchley or in Tooting anyway. The cliffs were far and away the best places for that sort of thing. There's a democracy of familic confusion out on these Cornish headlands – nobody else knows who he is either.

I am still surprised by how cheerfully I drove back here, the wind before me, the Fuglemans and the Flatmans behind. I was in such prime condition that I ought really to have stopped off at Paddington before I left London and gone looking for Melpomene. But I was eager to be away. I sailed along the motorway, acknowledging the friendly waves of lorry drivers and traffic police alike. For the first time ever I crossed the Tamar without a qualm. I didn't even mind those last, normally spirit-breaking fifteen miles, the ones that tell you you really are leaving the kindly concessions of social man. I whistled down those blind lanes with my windows open, and slowed the car right down to enjoy the spectacle of that ultimate upward sweep of land, its final flourish before dropping sheer into the sea.

I wasn't in a hurry to seek out the manilla envelope that Harry Vilbert had posted into my unused garden shed, but of course I was curious enough about it to have remembered it was there. The rats hadn't got it, but the damp very nearly had. I reckon the odd snake had tossed it around a bit also. The envelope was just about legible. It read, *What I think of my Husband*. And its contents were still legible too. I suppose it was inevitable that they would not contain a single reference to Thomas Hardy. *I* was the husband that Camilla wanted to express her thoughts about.

I don't know what effects this composition would have had upon my peace of mind had I read it when I was intended to – last autumn. I'm sure it would have set my convalescence back by months. But I'm stronger now, as I've proved. I read what Camilla had to say, then I walked down with it through the village, smiling and nodding as I went, out into the harbour, past the Museum and the harbour master's cottage, and up on to the cliffs. Once there I made for one of my most favourite vertiginous ledges, where I sat awhile and peered down into that absurd fuss and ferment below me; then, choosing my current of air as craftily as if I were a kestrel, I up-ended Camilla's envelope and let the pages of what she thought of her husband hang and sway for a moment before floating down with a rocking motion into the opal and the sapphire of that wandering western sea.

10. Lưu Trần Tiêu – Ngô Văn Doanh – Nguyễn Quốc Hùng. *Giữ gìn những kiệt tác kiến trúc trong nền văn hóa Chăm*, Nhà xuất bản Văn hóa dân tộc, Hà Nội, 2000.

NHÀ XUẤT BẢN THẾ GIỚI
46 Trần Hưng Đạo - Hà Nội - Việt Nam
Tel: 0084-4-8253841; Fax: 0084-4-8269578;
Mail: thegioi@hn.vnn.vn ;
Website: www.thegioipublishers.com.vn

Thánh địa Mỹ Sơn

Chịu trách nhiệm xuất bản:
TRẦN ĐOÀN LÂM

Biên tập :   Đông Vĩnh
Bìa: Lê Bích Thủy
Sửa bản in: Lê Hương
Trình bày: Hoàng Hoài

In 1000 bản, khổ 11x20cm, tại Trung tâm Chế bản và In - Nhà xuất bản Thế Giới. Giấy chấp nhận đăng ký kế hoạch xuất bản số 276-2008/CXB/28-50/ThG cấp ngày 2/4/2008. In xong và nộp lưu chiểu Quý III năm 2008.

TABLE DES MATIÈRES

Remerciements 9
Préface de Joëlle de Gravelaine 11
En souvenir de Maria Callas 15

PREMIÈRE PARTIE
LA VOIX

La voix humaine 19
Les motivations de ma recherche 21
Cette voix qui nous trahit 27
Voix et symboles du corps 39
L'impact sexuel de la voix 43
S'entendre, écouter 49
Je chante faux : est-ce irrémédiable? 54
La rééducation 64
Les problèmes de l'enseignant 78

DEUXIÈME PARTIE
CORPS ET VOIX

Ce que je propose 85
Le surdoué vocal 91
L'aspect correctif 94
L'ouverture, la déconstruction laryngée 96
Les muscles de l'articulation 101
  Muscles de la face. La langue. Les pommettes. Le nez. Le voile du palais. La mâchoire inférieure.
Les muscles de soutien 119
  Muscles du cou. La nuque, le dos. L'appareil phonatoire.
Les muscles de la phonation 131
Les micros de la voix 136
Muscles de la respiration : le souffle 138
Le mécanisme phonatoire 145
  La production sonore. Les registres et leurs passages. La puissance vocale. La couverture des sons. Les résonateurs. Le vibrato. Le système nerveux.

TROISIÈME PARTIE
LE CHANT

Le positionnement	185
Les salles	192
Les aventures du diapason	197
Enseigner le chant	203
Apprendre	210
La mélodie, le lied	213
Classification des voix	215
Quelques acrobaties vocales	220

QUATRIÈME PARTIE
LA TECHNIQUE

Avertissement	227
Quelques recommandations	228
Présentation des différents mouvements employés dans la gymnastique.	
La gymnastique vocale	239
La vocalisation	252
Effets sûrs et effets présumés de la technique	265
Bibliographie	269

Cet ouvrage a été composé et achevé d'imprimer pour les Éditions
Robert Laffont à Paris par l'Imprimerie Floch à Mayenne
le 5 mars 1985

Dépôt légal : décembre 1984. N° d'éditeur : L 378 (22849)

been against the idea from the start.'

Heller has been told on numerous occasions that he hasn't written another novel as good as *Catch-22*. He has a very simple reply: 'Who has?'

Subject index

Accounts, 130–3
Amplification/attenuation, 6, 265
Appreciation, 3, 30, 32
Ascribed rule-breaking, 12
Auto-involvements, 36, 75, 269
Avoidance-of-provocation, 239–249

Careers, 24, 250, 259
Causal structure, 159, 200, 238
Concealment strategies, 123ff
Criminological model, 21–3, 26, 33, 252

De-typing, 153ff; and re-typing, 156f
Deviance-imputations, 23f, 49, 55f, 93f, 142; categories of, 49–52; definition of, 52; and instructions, 53f; recognition of, 51f

Effectiveness/efficiency of treatment, 231f, 235
Elaboration, stage of, 145, 152ff, 171ff; *see also* Idiosyncratization, Motive elaboration, Type extension, Verification
Evidential strategies, 117–21; interrogative, 121f; as treatment, 235

Filling in, 55f, 58ff, 134ff

Functionalists, 221f, 250

Idiosyncratization, 158
Interpretive work, *see* Rules, evidential, interpretive
Irremediality, 188–90, 201–3, 210–15, 240f

Labelling theory, 3–16; general criticisms, 6f; phenomenological criticisms, 10–16; symbolic interactionist criticisms, 8–11
Likeability, 145, 190, 213f

Morality, principle of, 221ff
Motive elaboration, 158f, 177ff, 186, 195f, 198ff, 208ff
Motives, 24, 158f, 167, 198–201, 208–10, 238f
Movement management, 257f

Neutralization, 14, 259
Newcomer status, 154–6, 167

Paradigms, 1–3, 6f, 11, 18, 25, 27, 30f
Participant-observation, 30
Phases, 65–93; clearing up, 84–6; entry and settling down, 67–75; exit, 86–9; lesson proper, 75–84; *see also* Subphases

281

Subject index

Phenomenologists, 1f, 7, 10–16, 18, 25, 27–32, 254–6
Positivists, 1f, 6, 10, 18, 24–6, 28
Postulate of adequacy, 29f, 34, 221
Postulate of logical consistency, 27f
Postulate of subjective interpretation, 29, 221
Pragmatism, principle of, 221ff

Qualitative methodology, 30

Reactions to deviance, chapter 8; intervention and treatment, 221ff; *see also* Avoidance-of-provocation, Morality, Pragmatism
Retrospective interpretation, 124f, 128, 193
Routine deviance, 23, 27, 49, 55f, 93f, 142, 219, 249, 252
Rules: ad hoc, 91f; classroom, 35ff; evidential, 117ff, of conviction, 118ff, retrospective conviction, 125ff, retrospective suspicion, 124ff, of suspicion, 119ff, type-congruency, 136ff, type-discrepancy, 134ff; implemental, 107ff, 253; institutional, 34f, 92f; interpretive, 59, 91, 116, 253, 268; multiphasic, 92; personal, 34, 36, 43; relational, 93, pupil-pupil, 93, 101–4, teacher-pupil, 93, 95–101; school, 33ff; situational, 34f; suspension of, 89f

Schools, selection of, 30f
Secondary deviation, 5, 247

Secret deviance, 8f
Self-fulfilling prophecy, 140f
Self-labelling, 8, 259
Settling down, 150, 154, 162, 173ff
Sibling phenomenon, 160–2, 167, 180, 184, 200, 253, 259f
Speculation, stage of, 145ff, 253; *see also* Sibling phenomenon, Staff discussion, Standing out
Stabilization, stage of, 145, 186ff, 253, 262; *see also* Type centralization and Type fusion
Staff discussion, 162–5, 180, 205
Standing out, 147ff, 159ff
Stigma, 13, 267
Subphases, 75ff; type 1, 75–8; type 2, 78–81; type 3, 81–3
Subreactional deviance, 168f, 173, 180, 226, 253, 256
Switch-signal, 65ff, 89f, 253

Task-phase, 65
Teachers: deviance-insulative, 260ff; deviance provocative, 260ff
Themes: movement, 46, 48; pupil-pupil relational, 46, 49; talk, 46ff; teacher-pupil relational, 46, 48f; time, 46, 49
Time-flow principle, 223ff
Type centralization, 188
Type extension, 157
Type fusion, 187f
Type permanence, 186
Type transcendence, 157
Type transformation, 186f, 194, 262
Typing, stages of, 145; *see also* Elaboration, Speculation, Stabilization

Verification, 152ff

282

brayed his loud opinions on the arrangement of items in a shop – the exact location of sweets in relation to bread – even as she praised him to others.

He ate massively, ol' Changez, and I encouraged him to have two helpings of coconut ice-cream, which he ate as if it were about to be taken from him. 'Have anything you like,' I said to all of them. 'D'you want dessert, d'you want coffee?' I began to enjoy my own generosity; I felt the pleasure of pleasing others, especially as this was accompanied by money-power. I was paying for them; they were grateful, they had to be; and they could no longer see me as a failure. I wanted to do more of this. It was as if I'd suddenly discovered something I was good at, and I wanted to practise it non-stop.

When everyone was there, and nicely drunk and laughing, Eva stood up and knocked on the table. She was smiling and caressing the back of Dad's head as she strained to be heard. She said, 'Can I have some quiet. Some quiet, please, for a few minutes. Everyone – please!'

There was quiet. Everyone looked at her. Dad beamed around the table.

'There's an announcement I must make,' she said.

'For God's sake make it, then,' Dad said.

'I can't,' she said. She bent to his ear. 'Is it still true?' she whispered.

'Say it,' he said, ignoring the question. 'Eva, everyone's waiting.'

She stood up, put her hands together and was about to speak when she turned to Dad once more. 'I can't, Haroon.'

'Say it, say it,' we said.

'All right. Pull yourself together, Eva. We are getting married. Yes, we're getting married. We met, fell in love, and now we're getting married. In two months' time. OK? You're all invited.'

She sat down abruptly, and Dad put his arm around her. She was speaking to him, but by now we were roaring our approval and banging the table and pouring more drinks. I raised a toast to them, and everyone cheered and clapped. It was a great, unsullied event. After this there were hours of congratulation and drinking and so many people around our table I didn't have to talk much. I could think about the past and what I'd been through as I'd struggled to locate myself and learn what the heart is. Perhaps in the future I would live more deeply.

And so I sat in the centre of this old city that I loved, which itself sat at the bottom of a tiny island. I was surrounded by people I loved, and I felt happy and miserable at the same time. I thought of what a mess everything had been, but that it wouldn't always be that way.

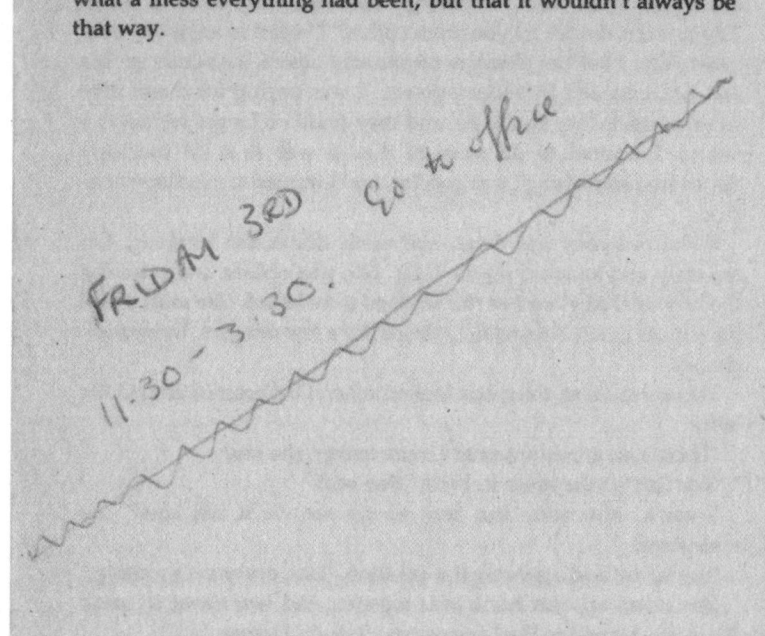

INDEX

Thames, river, 47, 54, 121, 123, 125, 126, 127, 136, 137, 138, 208, 214, 215, 231
Their Good Names (Hyde), 102
Thick, Detective Sergeant William, 77–8, 79
Thirty-third Masonic degree, 153–4, 161
Thomas, Danford, 217
Thompson, Sir Basil, 121
Thompson and McKay, Messrs, 217
Thorpe, Essex, 187
Thorpe-le-Soken, Essex, 186, 187, 197, 209
Thrawl Street, Spitalfields, 53, 114, 143, 144
Thyne, Dr Thomas, 133
Tilbury, 65
Times, The, 57, 66, 82, 169, 175, 198, 204, 205, 209, 238, 242, 243, 252
Tite Street, Chelsea, 138–9
Tottenham, 76
Tottenham Court Road, 25
Tottenham Street, 29
Toughill, Thomas, 138
Tower of Babel, 152
Trafalgar Square, 28, 81, 83, 84
Tranby Croft scandal, 86–8
Treasury, the, 117, 122
Truman's Brewery, Hanbury Street, 54
Truman, Hanbury and Buxton, 53
'Trunk of a Female', 50
Truth, 90
Turner, Martha – *see* Tabram, Martha
Turner, William, 217
Tyler, George, 76, 77, 78, 80

Union Lodge, 176
University of London, 181, 188

Vatican, the, 152
Veck, 115–18
Venice, 249
Venturney, Julia, 70
Vestry Hall, Cable Street, 241
Victims file (Scotland Yard), 49
Victoria Embankment, 138

Victoria Home, Commercial Street, 114
Victoria Street, Westminster, 18, 73
Victoria, Queen:
  mentioned, 17, 24, 43, 82, 93, 188, 191, 197, 210, 253
  fury over Eddy's marriage to Annie Elizabeth Crook, 27
  unpopularity, 28, 86, 89–90
  relations with family, 33
  letter to Gladstone, 81
  Golden Jubilee, 86, 89
  and Eddy's proposed marriage to Hélène d'Orléans, 91–2
  and Cleveland Street scandal, 117–18
  and Nichols murder, 141–2
  Lees called before, 195
  depicted in *Ennui*, 257
Vienna, 89, 156, 190
Vienna Observatory, the, 156
Vivisection, 191–2
Vollon, A., 260

Wales, 35
Walsh, Inspector, 73
Warren, Sir Charles:
  mentioned, 62
  and Kelly, 66
  appointed Commissioner, 84, 251
  and unemployed, 84
  and Freemasonry, 154–6, 160, 261
  and writing on wall, 160, 177–8
  resigns, 235
  and Packer, 245, 250
  and grapes in Stride murder, 244–6, 250, 261
  and Monro, 247
  and Anderson, 251
Watergate conspiracy, the, 107
Watkins, P.C., 60, 64
'Watt, Detective Chief Superintendent John', 18, 149, 150
Weaver's Arms, Hanbury Street, 177
Weber, Dr Hermann, 201
Wembley, Middlesex, 195
Wentworth Dwellings, Goulston Street, 177, 261

Wentworth Street, Whitechapel, 80
West, Acting Superintendent J., 77
West Country, the, 135
Westfield View, Rotherham, 231
Westminster Abbey, 44, 73
Westminster Board of Guardians, 98
Westminster Bridge, 40, 73, 214
Westminster Bridge Road, 122
Westminster Hospital, 215
Westminster Pier, 214, 215
Westminster Union, 42
What Does She Do With It?, 90
What Shall We Do For The Rent? (Sickert) – see *Camden Town Murder* series
Whistler, James McNeill, 25, 139
White, Sergeant Stephen, 243–5
Whitechapel, 15, 20, 34, 35, 51, 65, 66, 76, 77, 80, 110–11, 122, 123, 125, 141, 142, 143, 144, 159, 174, 184, 185, 205, 206, 207, 208–9, 221, 227, 228, 235, 261
Whitechapel Mortuary, 50, 52, 55, 167, 168
Whitechapel Road, 50, 52, 53, 59, 108
Whitechapel Vigilance Committee, 63, 121, 222, 242
Whitefriars Street, City, 52
Whitehall, 18, 27, 177
Whitehall Mystery, the, 125

White House, Flower and Dean Street, 144
White's Row, Spitalfields, 143
Whittington-Egan, Richard, 211
Wilde, Oscar, 81, 139
Wilks, S., 181–2, 200
William Withey Gull, A Biographical Sketch (Acland), 181
Williams, Watkin, 155
Wilson, Arthur, 87
Wilson, Colin, 135, 136, 180, 186, 206
Wilson, Mrs Arthur, 87
Wimborne, Dorset, 128
Winchester College, 128
Windsor, 30, 40, 56
Wingrove, Charles, 265
Winslow, Sarah, 95
Wiseman, Cardinal Nicholas, 91
Wood, Robert, 256
Woodford Green, Essex, 72
Workhouses, 98–101
Working Lads' Institute, Whitechapel Road, 108, 209
World's Tragedy, The (Crowley), 103
Worshipful Company of Fishmongers, the, 163
Writing on the wall, the, 61, 62, 177–8, 245, 261

X's Affiliation Order (Sickert), 255

'Y' DIVISION, 76
Yellow Palace, the, 43

Ben Weatherstaff's duties rarely took him away from the gardens, but on this occasion he made an excuse to carry some vegetables to the kitchen, and being invited into the servants' hall by Mrs Medlock to drink a glass of beer, he was on the spot – as he had hoped to be – when the most dramatic event Misselthwaite Manor had seen during the present generation actually took place.

One of the windows looking upon the courtyard gave also a glimpse of the lawn. Mrs Medlock, knowing Ben had come from the gardens, hoped that he might have caught sight of his master, and even by chance of his meeting with Master Colin.

'Did you see either of them, Weatherstaff?' she asked.

Ben took his beer-mug from his mouth and wiped his lips with the back of his hand.

'Aye, that I did,' he answered with a shrewdly significant air.

'Both of them?' suggested Mrs Medlock.

'Both of 'em,' returned Ben Weatherstaff. 'Thank ye kindly, ma'am, I could sup up another mug of it.'

'Together?' said Mrs Medlock, hastily overfilling his beer-mug in her excitement.

'Together, ma'am,' and Ben gulped down half of his new mug at one gulp.

'Where was Master Colin? How did he look? What did they say to each other?'

'I didna' hear that,' said Ben, 'along o' only bein' on th' step-ladder lookin' over th' wall. But I'll tell thee this. There's been things goin' on outside as you house people knows nowt about. An' what tha'll find out tha'll find out soon.'

And it was not two minutes before he swallowed the last of his beer and waved his mug solemnly towards the window which took in through the shrubbery a piece of the lawn.

'Look here,' he said, 'if tha's curious. Look what's comin' across th' grass.'

When Mrs Medlock looked she threw up her hands and gave a little shriek, and every man and woman servant within hearing bolted across the servants' hall and stood looking through the window with their eyes almost starting out of their heads.

Across the lawn came the Master of Misselthwaite, and he looked as many of them had never seen him. And by his side, with his head up in the air and his eyes full of laughter, walked as strongly and steadily as any boy in Yorkshire – Master Colin!

Arthur and the others were inspecting the wreckage and tutting at the devastation she slipped into the cellar and hunted till she found what she sought.

On a moonless, May night, when the stars blazed in the heavens, she took leave of her family and made her way up the hill to the overgrown chambers of the old squirrel colony. With the starlight burning on her brow she took a small pendant from the pocket of her dress and held it up to the celestial lamps. Their white fire flickered over the silver acorn in her paw and then Audrey tied it round her neck and her beauty was that of another world. With a sad smile on her lips she became the new Starwife, Handmaiden of Orion.

THE DEPTFORD MICE

Follow the adventures of the Deptford Mice in these three exciting stories:

The Dark Portal	£3.50	☐
The Crystal Prison	£3.50	☐
The Final Reckoning	£3.99	☐

Also by Robin Jarvis
The Whitby Witches (available April 1991)   £3.99   ☐

All Simon & Schuster Young Books are available at your local bookshop or can be ordered direct from the publisher. Just tick the titles you want and fill in the form below. Prices and availability subject to change without notice.

Simon & Schuster Cash Sales Department, PO Box 11, Falmouth, Cornwall, TR10 9EN, England.

Please enclose a cheque or postal order to the value of the cover price and allow the following for postage and packing:
UK: 80p for the first book, and 20p for each additional book ordered up to a maximum charge of £2.00.
BFPO: 80p for the first book, and 20p for each additional book.
OVERSEAS & EIRE: £1.50 for the first book, £1.00 for the second book, and 30p for each subsequent book.

Name ....

Address ....

....

Postcode ....

was as if they were sickening for the Sierra. I could believe it. I could believe anything by now.

I nearly chucked them away, but I didn't. They were a gift, a memento, evidence that I hadn't been dreaming. Now they're sitting on the customs man's desk. They're what this story, this whole business, is about. Behind all the greed and the violence, the need to make laws and the itch to break them, there is just this handful of leaves, medicine for the journey.

AUTHOR'S NOTE

Many people contributed to this story, some knowingly, some not. Almost all who appear in it do so with their names changed, and for obvious reasons some of them would not feel much thanked if I gave their real names now.

For particular help and encouragement before, during and after my trip to Colombia in 1983 I would like to thank the following: Luz Marina Vallejo, Ana, Dario, Raúl, Jaime and Estella Vallejo, Ana Rita and Juan Contreras, Nydia and Kevin Scanlan, Luis Murcia, David Godwin, Andrew Baldwin, Tony and Blanca Hutchings, Mary Ensor, Elena Vitterli, Giovanni, Alejandra Duarte, José and Olivia at Los Idolos, Omar Parodi, Jaime Conde Danies, Marc Gerstein, Chuck Pinsky, Garman Daza, Harvey and Clavia Aronson, Timothy Davis and Alastair Macdonald.

The mention of their names carries no suggestion of their involvement in, or approval of, cocaine. This book is not a tract for or against the trafficking of drugs. It is simply a story.

I know that I owe some sort of apology to the people of Colombia, because like everyone I talk of little else but their *mala fama*. I can only say that the book grew – if at an odd angle – out of my love for Colombia, and for the warmth, wit and honesty of its people.

saw there were men at work on the dancehall. It looked like they were readying it for demolition. There was an architect's sign that said there were going to be apartments built in due course. The hall itself looked almost ridiculously small, the hump of corrugated iron behind, the front itself that must indeed have once been a seaside dwelling. The flag was gone that once would have said the name, but in later years someone had affixed five iron letters to the front, now all greyed and rusted: P-L-A-Z-A. It was extraordinary for me to think of all the vanished history of this place. To think of Eneas McNulty walking here in his burned uniform, of Tom going in with his instruments, of the cars coming out from Sligo along the glistening strand, and the strains of music leaking out into the untrustworthy Irish summer air, and maybe straying even as far as the ancient ears of Queen Maeve. Certainly the ears of listening Roseanne, in her own buried exile.

It was more difficult to locate her hut. I found I had already passed the spot where it must have been, because I was able to find the fine wall of the big house across from it, and the gate where Jack's wife had humiliated Roseanne. At first I thought it was all just brambles and ruin, but the old stone chimney was still almost intact, though covered in lichen and climbing weeds. The rooms where Roseanne had lived out her sentence of living death were no more.

I walked in the ruined gap of the little gate and stood on the scruffy grass. There was nothing to see but in my mind's eye I could see everything, because she had supplied the ancient cinema of this place. Nothing except a neglected rose bush among the brambles, with a few last vivid blooms. Despite my reading of Bet's books, I found that I didn't know the name of it. But hadn't Roseanne mentioned it? Something, something . . . For the life of me, I couldn't remember what she had written. But I pushed forward through the thorns and weeds, thinking I might take a few blooms of it back to Roscommon as a souvenir. All the blooms were uniform, a neat tight-curled rose, except on one branch, whose roses were different, bright and open. I could feel the brambles tearing at my legs, and pulling at my jacket like beggars, but suddenly I knew what I was doing. I carefully peeled off a sprig as recommended in the books in the chapters on propagation, and slipped it in my pocket, feeling almost guilty, as if I were stealing something that didn't belong to me.

Index

early communication stage of communication 74
educational facilitation
  social world expansion 244–5
  feeding time 241–2
  fine motor skills 242–3
  personal hygiene 243–4
  photo albums 264
  as positive diversion 263
  reading with dogs 259–63
  road safety 257
  in school 258–60
  separation from dog 258
  sleeping arrangements 253–4
  social skills 255
  social world expansion 244–5, 264–7
  toilet training 246–52
  and transitional planning 239–41
  walking dogs 255–7
Equality Act (2010) 98
Erdwin, Maureen 27, 54
exercising dogs 37, 150, 169–71, 278

families
  benefits of dog ownership 31–3
  bonding with dog 151–2
  parental work patterns 36
  transition planning with 104–5, 108
feeding time 162–7, 241–2, 279–80
fine motor skills 242–3
fireworks 198–9
fleas 175
Friend Like Henry, A (AFLH) (Gardner) 10, 25, 26, 34, 61
Friendly Access 31

garden poisons 192–5
Gardner, Amy
  and cuddly dog 109
  death of Henry 274, 291, 298–300
  impact of Henry on 303–4
  love of horses 26, 244
  and public access dogs 46
  toilet training 247, 248–9
  transition planning with 107, 108

Gardner, Dale
  age appropriateness of 27–8
  choosing Henry for 40, 91–3, 94, 126
  commands for Henry 204–5, 207
  death of Henry 61–2, 267–70, 274, 286–8, 292–3
  educational facilitation through Henry 239–40, 241–6, 247, 251–2, 253–4, 258, 259–60, 263–5
  exercising Henry 169, 170, 171
  eye contact with Henry 53
  feeding time for Henry 166
  and Henry as older dog 284–5
  impact of Henry on 23–4, 25, 26, 33, 40, 303–4
  neutering of Henry 156
  playtime with Henry 172
  toilet routine of Henry 167
  transition planning with 48–9, 99, 102–3, 106–8, 109, 113
  world of autism 58
Gardner, Nuala
  and Andy MacGillivray 67, 68
  development of programme 26–33
  research on dogs and autism 17–18
Garrett, Heather 63–5
Goodman, J.F. 28
Grandgeorge, Marine 28, 91, 243
Grandin, Temple 253
grooming 116, 156–9, 278
Guide Dogs Queensland (GDQ) 29, 46, 117, 126
Guide Dogs UK 99, 129

Halti 122
harnesses 118–19, 149
health of dog 128–9
  Babesiosis 178
  bathing 158
  bloat 202–3
  ear cleaning 157–8
  exercise 37, 150, 169–71
  feeding time 162–7

fireworks 198–9
fleas 175
grooming 116, 156–9
heatstroke 200–1
Lyme disease 178
nail trimming 158
neutering 37, 155–6
older dogs 277–85
parasites 179–82
physical examinations 159–62
playtime 172–3
poisoning 182–98
stings 201
teeth 157, 158–9
ticks 175–7
toilet routine 167–9
vaccinations 174–5
veterinary care 38, 134, 174–5
vomiting 182
heart disease 281
heartworms 181–2
Heather 63–5
heatstroke 200–1
Heaven (Allan) 270, 273
Henry (One and Two) 34
  choosing 40, 91–3, 94, 126
  commands for 204–5, 207
  death of 61–2, 267–70, 274, 286–8, 292–3
  educational facilitation 239–40, 241–6, 247, 251–2, 253–4, 258, 259–60, 263–5
  exercising 169, 170, 17
  eye contact with Dale 53
  feeding time 166
  impact on Dale 23–4, 25, 26, 33, 40, 303–4
  neutering of 156
  as older dog 284–5
  playtime 172
  toilet routine 167
  transition planning for 48–9, 99, 102–3, 106–8, 109, 113
home
  considerations for dogs 36
  introducing dog to 69
  planning for dog's arrival 131–5
  poisons in 184–96
  settling dog into 148
hookworms 179

Human-Animal Bond Research Institute (HABRI) 32

intentional communication 73
International Guide Dog Federation 50
Irish Guide Dogs 111
Isaacs, James 53
Issacs, Wendy 53–4

Kefford, Jane 52
Keill, Valerie 26
Kennel Club 54, 92, 93, 126, 127
Kongs 119–21, 172
Kortabarria, Eneko 30–1

leads 117–18, 149
legal responsibilities 37, 152–3
lungworms 180–1
Lupien, Sonia 109
Lyme disease 178

MacGillivray, Andy 66–9
MacGillivray, Duncan 66–9
MacGillivray, Jenny 66–7, 68
Mahe 53
McLean, Shona 300
medicines as poisons 188–9
Millman, S.T. 47, 48
Mills, Daniel 32, 207
MIRA Foundation 109
Morris, Glynn 31

nail trimming 158
National Autistic Society (NAS) 22, 98, 286, 294–5, 296–7
neutering 37, 155–6
nicotine 196

older dogs 277–85
onions 185
'own agenda' stage of communication 74

PAAT 29, 46, 257
parasites 179–82
parents
   training assistance fogs 54
   working patterns of 36
Parents Autism Workshops and Support (PAWS) programme 99
partner stage of communication 74
personal hygiene 243–4
pets
   mixing with dogs 36
   and programme principles 20–1
phobia of dogs 36, 59

photo albums 264
physical examinations 159–62
plant poisons 190–2
playtime 172–3, 237
poisoning 182–98
potpourri 198
pre-intentional communication 73
public access dogs 45–6, 50, 51–3
puppy crates 133–4, 150–1

reading with dogs 259–63
Rederfer, L.A. 28
requester stage of communication 74
rewards in training 222–3, 225, 226, 233–4
road safety 257
Rodriguez, Mylos 30
roundworms 179

school
   assistance dogs in 258–60
Scottish Outdoor Access Code 153
Scriven, Colum 260–3
seasonal canine illness (SCI) 198
senior dogs 277–85
sensory issues 79–82, 112, 114–15
Service Dogs Canada 117
sleeping arrangements 133, 253–4, 281–2
Snow Cake (film) 275
social behaviour 234–6
social skills of child 255
social world of child 244–5, 264–7
socialising dogs 141–2, 143–5
songs 122–3
sourcing a dog 40–1, 56, 60, 125–30
stings 201
stress in dogs
   prevention 140–3
   signs of 137–40

tapeworms 180
Taylor, Jim 274
teeth of dogs 157, 158–9, 280–1
ticks 175–7
toads 192
toilet pen 132
toilet routine 167–9, 281
toilet training for child 246–52
towels 121

training
   assertiveness in 221
   attention of dog in 222, 230–1
   body language in 222
   clicker training 236
   commands in 221, 230–4
   confidence in 220
   consistency in 221
   corrections in 227–30
   dog psychology 219
   excitability of dog 235–6
   jumping up 234–5
   motivation in 224–7
   perseverance in 220
   personality of dog 226
   playtime 237
   positive reinforcement in 223–4
   positivity in 220
   praise in 224–7, 233–4
   puppies 134
   reasons for home training 49–54
   respect of dog 220
   responsibility for 223
   rewards in 222–3, 225, 226, 233–4
   social behaviour 234–6 *see also* commands
transitional kit 102–23
transitional planning
   and assistance dogs 99–100
   benefits of 48–9
   educational facilitation 239–41
   as first stage 58–9, 87–90
   importance of 98–101
   transitional kit for 102–23
treats 142–3

University of Lincoln 32

vaccinations 174–5
veterinary care 38, 134, 174–5, 282
vomiting 182

walking dogs 150, 152–3, 255–7
welfare of dogs
   importance of 40, 46–8
   rights to 96
   stress in dogs 137–43
whipworms 179
Wing, Lorna 22
working dogs 42–3

Xylitol 186

denn? was denn? Halt, ich schlag' einmal im Schellerschen
Lexikon auf: Universität, Akademie. Der letztere Ausdruck, der
freilich nicht ganz das besagt, was der erste, hat doch was Vor‍nehmeres, Brillanteres. „Ăcădēmiă, æ. f. 1. ein angenehmer,
schattigter Ort bei Athen — hier stand das berühmteste Gym‍nasium. 2. Dieses Gymnasium selbst, hier lebte und disputierte
Plato etc. — Änderungen erlitt — daher Academia vetus, Aca‍demia nova". Halt! Das ist just auf meine Mühle! Die bis‍herige wäre also die weiland Tübinger Academia, die vetus; die
Stuttgarter wäre die nova! Vortrefflich! Diese Distinktion hat zwar
ursprünglich einen anderen Sinn, überhaupt weiß ich nicht, wie
das hierher gehört, tut aber lediglich nichts, man kann die Leute
erstaunlich prellen. Definition ist Definition. Weiter heißt es:
Quaestiones Academicae. So könnt' ich mein Schriftchen titulieren.
Und da ist noch ein guter Einfall, ich setze alle äußern und
inneren Umstände, wodurch ich hiermit zum Schriftsteller ge‍worden, als Vorrede voran, die zwar etwas lang ist, weswegen
aber eben das Werkchen selber desto kürzer sein darf, denn es
kommt in der Welt bei Sachen der Art nicht darauf an, daß etwas
wirklich gesagt wird, sondern das Räuspern und Schwadronieren
ist alles. Ich fange an.

Terre'Blanche, Eugene 172
Theoane, Mashake 95
third-force theory 116-17
Thokoza township 13, 117, 162, 164
  dead zone 111, 118-19, 184, 198, 262, 270
  death toll 109
  described 109-10
  the elections 228, 231-3
  Ken's death *see under* Oosterbroek, Ken
  Lusaka section 113-14
  Mandela section 113
  monument to the dead 270-1
  recovery from the bloodshed 270
  Slovo section 113, 119
  taxis 121
  women killers in 56-7
Tillum, Guy 134
Time Magazine 132, 156, 157, 215, 235, 249, 250, 253
toyi-toyi (militant dance) 124
train killings ix, x
Transkei 112
Troyeville, Johannesburg 143, 245
Truth and Reconciliation Commission 99, 267-70
  report (1998) 95, 269
Tshabalala, Lindsaye, death of 29-40, 43, 45
tsotsis 26, 119-20, 122
tsotsitaal (township slang)
  xiv, 25, 110
Tswana 167
Tutsis 183, 256
Tutu, Archbishop Desmond ix-xii, 103
  leads the Truth and Reconciliation Commission 267

Ulundi 111, 113, 198
Umkhonte we Sizwa 284
Union Buildings, Pretoria 233
United Democratic Front 115
United Democratic Movement 282
United Nations
  forces in Mozambique 250
  Kevin and Joao's trip to Sudan 142-6
  Operation Lifeline Sudan project, Girgiri 141, 143, 192-3
United States, low tolerance for violent images 38-9

Vaal Monster *see* Kheswa, Victor Khetisi
Vaal River 100
Vaal Triangle 100, 101
Velasco, Paul 141, 185
Ventersdorp 170
Vereeniging 54
vierkleur flag 185
Vietnam 71
Viljoen, General Constand 171, 175, 178
Vlakplaas police unit 118

Weekly Mail 53, 104, 135, 141, 144, 161, 251
Weinberg, Paul 134
Western Transvaal 171
White City 24
white right, heartland of 171
white supremists
  and Bophuthatswana 170-1
  and the negotiated settlement with Mandela 172
  terror campaign by 185
Witbank 170
Wolfaardt, Alwyn 179
World 133
Wulfsohn, Giselle 134

Xhosa language 137-8
Xhosa tribe 21-2
  intelezi ceremony 135-8
  and Khalanyoni hostel 112
  and Khumalo 136-9
  in Phola Park squatter camp 55, 112
  warriors of Mandela Park 135-6

Yugoslav army 64
Yugoslavia, former 42, 67, 212
Zaire 249, 256, 261
Zimbabwe 9
zombies 107-8, 124, 125, 271
Zulu language 137-8
Zulus 3
  and Boipatong massacre 95-8
  civil war moves to the Reef 15-16
  fiery death of a Zulu (Tshabalala) 29-40, 43, 45
  forging of Zulu nation 86
  in migrants' hostels 15-18
  murder of Stanley Rapoo 89-93
  and the police 116
  rural dialect 32
  rural ties 112
  social alienation 86
  treatment of non-Zulu 18-23
  war cry ('Usuthu!') 16, 110
  warrior groups 113
  weapons 95, 109, 113
Zwane, Aubrey 73-4
Zwane, Jeremiah 73

Scytosiphon lomentaris 24, 25
Seeanemonen 74
Seefächer 84, 85
Seefedern 82
Seegräser 44
Seegurken 242
Seehase 148, 149
Seehecht 268, 269
Seeigel 236
Seekuckuck 274, 275
Seemaßliebchen 76, 77
Seemaus 98, 99
Seenadel, Große 272, 273
Seeohren 126
Seepapagei 286, 287
Seepeitsche 82, 83
Seepferdchen 272
Seepocken 184
Seequirl 26, 27
Seeratte 262, 263
Seerinde 224, 225
Seeringelwürmer 104
Seescheiden 248
Seeschmetterling 290, 291
Seespinne, Große 218, 219
Seestachelbeere 86, 87
Seesterne 230
Seetraube 20, 21
Seewalze, Finger- 242, 243
Segelqualle 68, 69
Sepia elegans 180
– officinalis 180, 181
Sepiola rondeleti 180, 181
Seriola dumerili 276, 277
Serpula vermicularis 116, 117
Serpulidae 116–119
Serranus cabrilla 274, 275
– hepatus 274, 275
– scriba 274, 275
Sertularia cupressina 64, 65
– gayi 64, 65
Sidnyum turbinatum 248, 249
Siebanemone, 76, 77
Siphonophora 68
Sipunculoidea 120
Sipunculus nudus 120, 121
Siriella clausii 190, 191
Solen marginatus 176, 177
Solecurtus strigillatus 176, 177
Solenocurtus strigillatus 176, 177
Sonnenmuschel, Rosige 176, 177
Sonnenrose 76, 77
Spadella cephaloptera 244, 247
Spargelkraut-Rotalge 30, 31
Sparisoma cretense 286, 287
Sparus auratus 278, 279
Spatangus purpureus 240, 241
Spermatochnus paradoxus 22, 23
Sphacelaria cirrhosa 26, 27
Sphaerechinus granularis 238, 239
Sphaerococcus coronopifolius 32, 33
Sphaeroma hookeri 192
– serratum 192, 193
Sphyraena sphyraena 270, 271
Sphyrna zygaena 260, 261
Spindel-Thyone 242, 243

Spindel, Zierliche 144, 145
Spinnentang, Gefranster 32, 33
Spionidae 108–109
Spirastrella cunctatrix 52, 53
Spirographis spallanzanii 114, 115
Spirorbis borealis 118, 119
– pagenstecheri 118, 119
Spisula subtruncata 172, 173
Spritzbrasse 280, 281
Spitzschnauzenhai 256, 257
Spondyliosoma cantharus 278, 279
Spondylus gaederopus 162, 163
Spongia officinalis 54, 55
Sporochnus pedunculatus 24, 25
Sprattus sprattus 264, 265
Springkrebse 206
Spritz-Ascidie 250, 251
Spritzwürmer 120
Sprotte 264, 265
Sproß-Ascidie 248, 249
Spurilla neapolitana 154, 155
Squalus acanthias 260, 261
– fernandius 260, 261
Squatina aculeata 260
– oculata 260
– squatina 260, 263
Squilla demaresti 188, 189
– mantis 188, 189
Staatsquallen 68
Stachelauster 162, 163
Stachelhäuter 228
Stachelhummer 204, 205
Stachelpolyp 60, 61
Stachelschnecke 142, 143
Stechrochen 262, 263
Steckmuscheln 160
Steinblatt 34, 35
Steinbohrer 178, 179
Steinbutt 304, 305
Steinköhler 268, 269
Steinkorallen 80, 81
Steinseeigel 238, 239
Sthenelais boa 98, 99
Sternascidie 252, 253
Sternaspididae 112
Sternaspis scutata 112, 113
Sterngucker 290, 291
Sternseepocke 184, 185
Stichopus regalis 242, 243
Stictyosiphon adriaticus 22, 23
Stieltang 24, 25
Stilophora rhizodes 22, 23
Stör 264, 265
Störartige 264
Stomatopoda 188
Strandflöhe 194
Strandkrabbe 214, 215
Strandkrebs 208, 209
Strandschnecken 132
Streifenbrasse 278, 279
Streifenlippfisch 286, 287
Streifenschleimfisch 292, 293
Strudelwürmer 88
Stumpen-Ascidie 250, 251
Stutzschnecke, Glatte 132, 133
Styela plicata 252, 253
Stylarioides eruca 110, 111
Stylochus pilidium 88, 89
Stylocidaris affinis 236, 237

Suberites domuncula 52, 53
Sycon ciliata 50, 51
– raphanus 50, 51
Syllidae 102–103
Syllis prolifera 102, 103
Synalpheus laevimanus 200, 201
Synascidien 248
Syngnathus acus 272, 273
– typhle 272, 273

Talitrus saltator 194, 195
Tanaidacea 188–189
Tange 28–34
Tanggras 44, 45
Tangrose 76, 77
Taonia atomaria 26, 27
Tapes decussatus 170, 171
Taschenkrebs 216, 217
Taschenmessermuschel 176, 177
Teleostei 264–305
Tellerqualle 68, 69
Tellina crassa 174, 175
– distorta 174, 175
– incarnata 174, 175
– planata 174, 175
– tenuis 174, 175
Tellmuscheln 174, 175
Tentaculata 86–87
Teppichmuscheln 170, 171
Terebellidae 114–115
Teredo navalis 178, 179
Tethya aurantium 52, 53
Tethys leporina 156, 157
Tetrastemma melanocephalum 92, 93
Thais haemastoma 142, 143
Thalassema gigas 120, 121
Thalassoma pavo 290, 291
Thaliacea 246–247
Thallophyta 16–43
Thecacera pennigera 150, 151
Thecata 62–67
Thecocarpus myriophyllum 66, 67
Thecocaulus diaphanus 66, 67
Thia polita 214, 215
– scutella 214, 215
Thorogobius ephippiatus 298, 299
Thracia papyracea 178, 179
Thune 302–304
Thunnus alalunga 302
– thynnus 302, 303
Thuridilla hopei 148, 149
Thyone fusus 242, 243
Thysanozoon brocchii 88, 89
Tintenfische 180
Tomopteridae 100–101
Tomopteris helgolandica 100, 101
Tonnenförmige Salpe 246, 247
Torpedo marmorata 260, 261
– nobiliana 260, 261
– torpedo 260, 261
Trachinus draco 290, 291
– vipera 290, 291
Trachinotus glaucus 278, 279
– ovatus 278, 279
Trachurus trachurus 276, 277
Trägerkrabbe 212, 213
Trapez, Kleines 164, 165

319

Trichteralge 26, **27**
Tricolia pullus 132, **133**
Trigla lyra 274, **275**
Tripterygion minor 294, **295**
– *nasus* 294, **295**
– *tripteronotus* 294, **295**
Trisopterus luscus 268, **269**
– *minutus capelanus* 268, **269**
Tritaeta gibbosa 196, **197**
Tritonschnecke 140, **141**
Tritonalia aciculata 142, **143**
Trivia adriatica 138, **139**
– *mediterranea* 138, **139**
– *monacha* 138, **139**
Trochus exasperatus 128, **129**
– *granulatus* 128, **129**
– *striatus* 128, **129**
Trogmuscheln 172, **173**
Trompetenanemone 76, **77**
Truncatella subcylindrica 132, **133**
Tubiclava fruticosa 60, **61**
Tubucellaria opuntioides 226, **227**
Tubulanus annulatus 90, **91**
– *nothus* 90
Tubularia indivisa 58, **59**
Turbanschnecke 130, **131**
Turbellaria 88–89
Turmschnecken 132–134
Turritella communis 134, **135**
– *triplicata* 132
Tylos sardous 194, **195**

Udotea petiolata 18, **19**
Ulva lactuca 16, **17**
– *linza* 16, **17**
Umbraculum mediterranea 146, **147**
Umbrina cirrosa 284, **285**
Upogebia deltaura 208, **209**
Uranoscopus scaber 290, **291**
Urochordata 246

Vadigo 276, **277**
Valonia utricularis 20, **21**

Velella velella 68, **69**
Venericardia sulcata 164, **165**
Venerupis decussata 170, **171**
– *pullastra* 170, **171**
– *rhomboides* 170, **171**
Ventromma halecioides 64, **65**
Venus ovata 170, **171**
– *striatula* 170, **171**
– *verrucosa* 170, **171**
Venusgürtel 86, **87**
Venusmuscheln 170, **171**
Veretillum cynomorium 82, **83**
Vermetus gigas 134, **135**
– *triqueter* 134
Verongia aerophoba 54, **55**
Verruca stroemia 184, **185**
Verrucaria adriatica 42, **43**
Vertebrates 254–305
Vidalia volubilis 40, **41**
Vielborster 94
Virgularia mirabilis 82, **83**
Vogelmuschel 160, **161**
Vorderkiemer 126

Wachsrose 74, **75**
Warzen-Ascidie 250, **251**
Warzenflechte 42, **43**
Warzen-Herzmuschel 168, **169**
Warzenmagelone 108, **109**
Warzenrose, Felsen- 74, **75**
Warzenschnecke, Mittelmeer- 146, **147**
Weichkorallen 84
Weichtiere 122
Weißgrundel 300, **301**
Wellhornschnecken 140
Wendeltreppe 136, **137**
Wespe, Mittelmeer- 70, **71**
Wimperkalkschwamm 50, **51**
Wirbeltiere 254
Wittlinge 266, **267**
Witwenrose 76, **77**
Wollkrabbe 212, **213**
Wolfsbarsch 276, **277**
Wrackbarsch 276, **277**

Würfelturban 130, **131**
Würmer, Marine 88
Wurmschnecken 132
Wurmseewalze 242, **243**
Wurmtang 30, 31
Wurzelalge 22, **23**
Wurzelkrebs, Parasitischer 186, **187**

Xantho floridus 216
– *hydrophilus* 216, **217**
– *incisus* 216
– *pilipes* 216, **217**
Xiphias gladius 304, **305**

Zackenbarsch, Brauner 276, **277**
Zahnbrasse 282, **283**
Zahnkrabbe 214, **215**
Zanklea costata 58, **59**
Zauberbuckel 130, **131**
Zeus faber 270, 271
Ziegenfisch 270, **271**
Zitterrochen 260, **261**
Zoantharia 72–73
Zoobotryon verticillatum 224, **225**
Zostera marina 44, **45**
– *nana* 44, **45**
Zosterissor ophiocephalus 299, **300**
Zottenplanarie 88, **89**
Zottentang 24, **25**
Zwergdorsch 268, **269**
Zwergflechte 42, **43**
Zwerg-Seegras 44, **45**
Zwergseeigel 240, **241**
Zwergsepia 180, **181**
Zylinderrosen 72
Zylinderschwamm, Farbwechselnder 54, **55**
Zypressenmoos 64, **65**

Avusturya 79, 83, 89, 107, 108, 138, 151, 155, 157, 166, 183, 198, 199, 280-283, 287, 291
Avusturya-Macaristan 19, 20, 42, 57, 59, 76, 79, 84, 88, 89, 91, 106, 108, 117, 119, 125, 154, 170, 187, 197, 198, 200, 201, 203, 278-283, 286-288, 290-292

Bağdad 176
Balkanlar 24, 28, 31, 39, 42, 45, 62, 63, 65, 94, 96, 113, 117, 125, 131, 154, 159, 161, 169, 176, 189, 205, 209-211, 214, 215, 221, 223, 224, 227-229, 231, 232, 235, 237, 239, 240, 242, 248-251, 255, 257, 259, 261, 263, 265, 267, 286
Berlin Antlaşması (1878) 122, 251, 281
Berlin Konferansı 259, 267, 268, 280
Besarabya 122, 214
Beyazıd 126, 252, 278
Bosna(-Hersek) 24, 42, 76-79, 89, 108, 118, 137, 177, 187, 200, 201, 203, 208, 212, 223, 224, 227, 228, 250, 257, 263, 266, 269, 270, 274, 278-283, 285, 287-291, 301
Boşnak 25, 58, 71, 73, 76-79, 99, 107, 125, 127, 128, 169, 186-188, 197-201, 203, 208, 219, 257, 278-280, 282-292
Bulgar Ayaklanması (*Aprilsko Vastanie*, 1876) 261
Bulgar(istan) 24, 29, 42, 48, 57, 58, 60, 62, 83, 89, 93, 94, 101, 111-114, 117, 120, 153, 197, 198, 208, 212, 215, 216, 223-225, 227, 228, 242, 249-251, 255, 257, 260-263, 265-268, 270-274, 278, 279, 282, 285, 288, 289

Canik (Samsun) 139, 174, 238
Canikli Ali Paşa (1720-1785) 238
Celalî isyanları 174
celb 118, 147, 186, 188, 210, 282, 284, 301
cemaat 22, 27, 30, 80, 81, 120, 127, 149, 294

Cengiz, -'in torunları 225, 259
Cezayir işgali 222
cihad 76, 186, 227, 240-242

Çar I. Aleksander 61, 230
Çeçen, Çeçenya 125, 126, 150, 152, 163, 166, 217, 234, 244, 252, 256
Çerkes, Çerkezistan 41, 44, 47, 50, 51, 56, 62, 93, 99, 103, 106, 113-115, 118, 125, 139-142, 146, 150-152, 160-164, 167, 168, 174, 183, 186-189, 192, 196, 197, 199, 202, 205, 208, 209, 212, 215-217, 219, 226, 227, 238-244, 246-255, 259, 261, 262, 274

Dağıstan 114, 118, 150, 187, 196, 208, 216, 234, 239, 248, 252, 274
Danimarka 183
Darphane 166
dârülharb 22, 25, 72-76, 79, 269
dârülislam 22, 25-27, 71-75, 79, 80, 87, 199
Derby, İngiliz Dışişleri Bakanı 249
Devlet-i Aliyye, Osmanlı Devleti, Babıâli 23, 49, 50, 54, 56, 60, 63-65, 72, 74, 76, 81, 83, 86, 88, 89, 91, 97, 101, 104, 108, 109, 111-113, 115-119, 123, 125-127, 130, 131, 133, 134, 136-141, 147, 150-152, 157, 160, 162, 166-168, 173, 176-178, 182, 184-188, 190-192, 196-198, 200, 202-204, 206, 208, 213, 215-219, 222, 223, 225-227, 237-244, 246-249, 251-253, 260, 266, 271-278, 281-288, 290, 292, 294, 295, 297, 299, 300
devlet-i ebed-müddet 68, 297
Dîn ü Devlet 21, 25, 26, 28, 29, 49, 68-70, 72, 170, 182, 186, 198, 199, 202, 219, 225-227, 247, 279, 283, 284, 290, 297
Dobruca 47, 139, 140, 158, 159, 192, 210, 215, 235-237, 247, 251, 255, 263
Doğu Anadolu 28, 116, 126, 153, 176, 204, 209, 216, 252, 260

Doğu Ortodoksları Koalisyonu 263
Doğu sorunu 153, 155

Edirne Antlaşması, 1829 131, 239
Eflak Boğdan 83, 109, 159, 222
Epir 249
Erdel (Moldovya ve Romanya) 222
Erivan gobernorate 160
Ermeni(istan) 38, 40, 51, 53, 81, 83, 89, 93, 94, 101, 102, 111, 112, 118, 122, 123, 160, 210, 215, 252, 260, 301
Erzurum 112, 126, 162, 211, 217, 252, 277
esir 93, 174, 196, 244
Eskişehir 169, 194
European concert (Avrupa dengesi) 154
ev göçü 174
Evpatoria 231, 235

Feodosia 235
Feodosia limanı 234
Ferah Ali Paşa 226, 239
Fırka-i Islahiye 99, 153, 160, 175, 178, 186
Filistin 31, 87, 97, 121, 139, 209, 212, 223, 228, 231
Fournier, Fransız konsolos 216
Fransa 20, 42, 53, 82, 84, 85, 100, 108, 117, 118, 143, 154-156, 158, 161, 170, 171, 183, 214-216, 222, 231, 242, 244, 249, 261, 271, 294

Gaspıralı İsmail Bey 28, 59, 104, 106, 119, 201, 202, 229, 236, 238, 298
gayrimüslim 22, 23, 25, 27, 28, 33, 45, 54, 57, 58, 63-65, 69, 72-76, 79-81, 83, 84, 86-88, 92, 94, 95, 101, 103, 112, 115, 120-122, 124, 128, 136, 138, 144, 176, 182, 185, 207, 209, 215, 223, 228, 246, 253-255, 257, 260, 270, 271, 285, 291, 297, 298, 300, 303
Gazi Bey 151, 152
Gazi Hasan Paşa, Kaptan-ı Derya 238
Gelibolu 184

Giray Hanedanı/Ailesi 225, 229
Girit Müslümanları 223, 295
Goltz Paşa 155
Gürcü, Gürcistan 93, 94, 105, 168, 223, 229, 239, 242, 257, 274-276

Habsburg 77, 108, 228, 285-287
hac ziyareti 128, 145, 151, 152
Hakkâri 211, 217, 252
Hamdi Bey 45, 257
Hazine-i Hassa Kumpanyası 135, 166, 167
Hıristiyan 47, 55, 57, 64, 69, 72, 74, 75, 81, 87-89, 92-97, 101-103, 109, 111, 112, 115, 121, 139, 143, 144, 164, 188, 196-198, 200, 201, 209, 213, 218, 228, 230, 234, 239, 246, 248, 254, 262, 263, 268, 271, 286, 289, 292-295, 298, 303
Hicaz 176
hicret/tehcir 21, 22, 25, 28, 31, 51, 53, 57, 67, 68, 71-79, 86, 98, 103-106, 115, 118, 119, 123, 137, 146, 153, 167, 186, 187, 193, 196, 199, 200, 202, 208, 211, 227, 229, 233, 240, 248, 253, 264, 267, 276, 277, 283, 290, 295, 299
Hüdavendigâr 117, 211

Iskat-ı cenin (kürtaj) 177, 178

İbrahim Bey 150, 183, 189
İdâre-i Umumiyye-i Muhâcirîn Komisyonu 142
İkdam gazetesi 45, 291
iltica 72, 88, 89, 97, 115, 121, 124, 228, 245, 258
İngilizler, İngiltere (Büyük Britanya) 61, 98, 100, 154, 155, 159-162, 202, 215, 227, 242, 244, 249, 251, 252, 268, 294
İran 24, 87, 93, 101, 118, 125, 174, 222, 228, 240, 258, 301
irtida 24, 71, 74, 96, 197, 292
İslâm Muhacirleri Komisyonu 142
İstambılak lueşhue [Çerkes 1864 Büyük Göçü] 246

Glossary

2	**hamlet:** a small village
4	**consul:** a government official sent abroad to look after people from his/her own country
12	**dislocated:** put out of joint
14	**state room:** a first class cabin
15	**plush:** richly luxurious
16	**knickerbockers:** a pair of short trousers
17	**juvenile:** young
18	**boa:** a long, thin feathery scarf
22	**mouldering:** rotting
26	**impertinent:** cheeky
27	**bandanna:** a large, coloured handkerchief
28	**customs:** a government organisation that collects taxes on goods taken in or out of a country
32	**fly-papers:** sticky papers to catch flies
43	**carbolic soap:** a strong, antiseptic soap
46	**skein:** a wound up length of yarn or thread
58	**ochre:** a pale brownish-yellow colour
61	**metronome:** an instrument that measures musical beats
62	**balefully:** menacingly
79	**piebald:** multicoloured
84	**dirndl:** a colourful, full skirt
86	**aristocracy:** upper classes, nobility
89	**blotched:** covered in large spots
102	**raked:** at an angle
106	**rakish:** jaunty
115	**guillotine:** a device that cuts off people's heads
116	**quelling:** repressing
127	**flogged:** whipped
139	**sanctuary:** a place of safety

150	**hoodwink:** to trick
155	**bilges:** the lowest parts of the inside of a boat
158	**pulmonary:** to do with the lungs
159	**assets:** possessions
161	**trespassing:** entering without permission
169	**furtively:** secretly
171	**leper colony:** a place where people with leprosy live
176	**poinsettia:** an indoor plant, popular at Christmas time
	askew: crooked
189	**hysterical:** uncontrolled emotion
192	**mantle:** a weight of responsibility
196	**deceased:** dead
203	**benzene:** a toxic chemical
205	**Primus:** a portable stove
214	**gout:** an inflammation of the joints, usually the big toe
216	**woebegone:** forlorn, in a sorry state
226	**henchman:** a follower of a criminal, a right-hand man
228	**septic:** infected
236	**bailiff:** a person employed to carry out orders
240	**calico:** a stiff, cotton cloth
252	**smoke inhalation:** damage done to lungs when smoke and heat is breathed in
261	**pilfered:** stolen
266	**anguished:** distraught, tormented
269	**machete:** a knife, axe
294	**termite:** a group of small, tropical insects
297	**ancestral:** inherited
	loitering: hanging around

İstanbul Anlaşması (Osmanlı-Yunan, 1897) 111, 269, 275, 295
İstanbul Konferansı/Anlaşması 111, 216, 269, 275, 295
istatistik 28, 44, 207, 208, 223, 237, 248, 262

Kabartay 141, 187, 214, 225, 240
Kadirilik 239
Kafkas/Kafkaslar/Kafkasya 24, 36, 41-45, 50, 53, 55, 56, 58, 60-63, 71, 72, 85, 92-96, 98, 99, 101, 102, 104-106, 111-115, 117, 120, 122, 125, 126, 129, 137, 139-141, 145-150, 152, 160-162, 165-168, 173, 182, 186, 188, 197, 199, 201, 202, 206, 208-214, 216, 217, 221-229, 231, 236-249, 252-262, 274, 276, 279, 290, 301
Karaçaylı 153
Karadağ 89, 250, 281
Karadeniz 41, 111, 112, 114, 115, 155-157, 161-163, 168, 179, 230-232, 240, 243, 246
karantina 176
Kayı 225, 259
Kazak 47, 48, 93, 95, 104, 182
kefalet sistemi 174
Kefe sancağı/beylerbeyliği 229
Kerch limanı 234
Kerç 112, 119, 159, 162, 168
Kezlev 231, 232
Kıbrıs 29, 144, 215, 216, 255, 269
Kırım (Aktopraklar) 24, 36, 39, 42, 43, 47, 48, 50, 51, 53, 56, 57, 59, 61-64, 67, 71, 72, 75, 85, 88, 91-96, 98, 99, 101, 102, 104-106, 109, 112, 113, 115, 117-120, 122, 129, 130, 136-141, 145-147, 149-154, 156-162, 164, 165, 167, 168, 179, 182, 186, 187, 189, 193, 194, 199, 201, 202, 208, 210, 214, 219, 221-239, 241, 242, 245-247, 249, 257-262, 279, 301
Kırım Hanlığı 221, 225, 226, 229, 238
Kırım Savaşı, 1853-1856 39, 47, 57, 59, 104, 105, 112, 118, 129, 130,
137-139, 153, 154, 156-158, 160-162, 164, 165, 186, 210, 224, 227-230, 237, 241, 242, 249, 261
koloni(ler) 61, 95, 98, 139, 150, 162, 183, 189, 238, 250, 286, 292
komitacılık 189, 248
Konya Savaşı 184
Kozak 225
köle 93, 121, 173, 174, 184, 219, 226
Kuban nehri 242, 274
Kundukhov, General Musa 152
Kuvve-i askeriye 24, 187, 278, 298, 301
Küçük Kaynarca, 1774 109, 155, 204, 223, 229, 238
küffar 226
Kürt 40, 45, 53, 185

Layard, İngiliz Büyükelçi 216, 249, 252
Leh 88, 102, 121, 223, 226
Londra protokolü (1877) 250
Ionescu-Brad, Ion, Romanyalı uzman 191
Lozan Anlaşması 30, 81
Lübnan 212, 261, 293

Macar 88, 121, 190, 223, 226, 287
Makedonya 28, 57, 94, 155, 210, 215, 223, 227, 228, 250, 251, 255, 260, 261, 266, 268, 269, 273, 282, 288, 289
Malahama, Rus General 152, 253
Malakanlar 94, 97, 223
Mecidiye Nişanı 127, 146, 153
Meclis-i Mebusan 45, 68
Meclis-i Umumi, Osmanlı 250
Meclis-i Vâlâ 137, 139, 146, 158, 232, 241, 244
Mehmed Ali Paşa, Kavalalı 80, 97, 183, 190
Memâlik-i (mahrûse-i) şâhâne 88, 118, 171, 208, 211, 212, 299
Memalik-i İslâmiye (Osmanlı) 225
Memalik-i Osmaniye 71, 125, 199, 240
Men-i Mürûr Nizamnamesi, 1841 174
metruk arazi 55, 135, 172, 175
Mısır 80, 97, 168, 176, 183, 190

Midhat Paşa 267
milis ordu 180, 182, 183
millet sistemi 79, 80, 82, 84, 298
millet-i hâkime 102
mirî 55, 79, 115, 124, 134, 135, 209, 241, 246, 290, 298, 299
mirza 120, 230
Moldovya 101, 166, 222, 231
Mora isyanı, 1821 179
Muhacir Komisyonu, 1860 45, 130, 136, 140-143, 233, 273, 276
Muhacir Nizamnamesi (1864) 212
mübadele 64, 110, 111, 113, 114, 116, 120, 121, 131, 246, 265-267, 271, 296
müftü 76, 77, 104, 105, 119, 120, 230, 284, 289
mülk ü millet 21, 25-29, 70, 225, 227, 290
mülteci(ler) 17, 18, 22, 26-28, 32, 37, 45, 48, 49, 64, 81, 85, 88-91, 121, 223
Müridizm hareketi 227, 239
Müslim/Müslüman 20, 22-25, 27-31, 33, 38, 42, 44, 45, 47-49, 54-59, 61-65, 67, 70-82, 84-88, 90-99, 101-106, 108-112, 114-126, 128, 130, 131, 136-140, 142-146, 151-154, 158, 159, 161-165, 168-170, 173, 175, 176, 178-182, 184, 185, 187-189, 193-199, 201-216, 218, 219, 221-225, 227-236, 238-244, 247-252, 254-267, 269, 271-279, 282, 283, 285-291, 293-303
Müslüman ve Sırp Ortak Delegasyonu, 1902 203, 290

nakl 72, 109, 113, 131
Nakşibendilik 32, 239, 302
Navarin 155, 179
nezr 174
nisbi(yet)/oran 26, 27, 51, 54, 59, 101, 106, 110, 116, 120, 134, 167, 173, 180, 183, 185, 188, 192, 204, 224, 225, 252, 254, 256, 261, 262, 265, 266, 269, 273, 277, 280, 292, 293, 295, 298

nizâm-ı âlem 297
Nogay 44, 50, 56, 113, 125-127, 142, 146, 150, 152, 153, 160, 167, 187, 189, 208, 212, 223, 233, 234, 237, 254
Novorossiysk 153

Ortodoks 74, 89, 92-94, 96, 97, 100, 103, 108, 114, 161, 197, 204, 230, 240, 263, 279, 287, 297
Osmanlı 15, 18-28, 31-33, 35, 36, 38-65, 67-76, 78-99, 101-147, 150-174, 176-179, 181-207, 209, 212, 214-219, 221-232, 234-259, 261-263, 265-291, 293-303
Osmanlı-Rus Anlaşması (1700) 47, 50
Osmanlı-Rus Savaşları:
    1787-1792 Savaşı 225, 230, 241
    1806-1812 Savaşı 241, 230
    1828-1829 Savaşı 112, 144, 179, 301
    1876-1877 Savaşı (93 Harbi) 45, 65, 86, 94, 99, 106, 111, 116, 125, 126, 142, 143, 147, 160, 163, 188, 215, 224, 227, 235, 239, 250, 252, 257, 259, 262-266, 270, 274, 275, 277, 278, 280
Osmanlı-Rus Tabiiyet Anlaşması (1862) 82
Osmanlıcılık 26, 28, 39, 82, 142, 258, 298

paganist 199
Panislâmizm (ittihad-ı İslâm) 188, 195, 203
Paris Anlaşması 21. Madde (1856) 233
Paris Konferansı/Anlaşması (1856) 62, 80, 130, 153-155, 202, 227, 228, 233, 242, 266, 274, 302
pasaport kanunu 81
Perekop 231, 232
Pomak 71, 99, 197, 198, 228, 257
Preveze 215, 216
Preveze Mükâlemesi (Osmanlı-Yunan) 216
Prusya 122, 138, 155, 183

to her antique armoire and the various relics from the Sistine Chapel are nothing that thousands of dollars and a couple of really good restorers in Florence can't repair. But seriously, what good luck it is for me to pay my rent each month (well, more or less) to a psychoanalyst who deals with whatever damage she finds as an indication of some sort of aggression that needs to be worked through in therapy. Jane has also become a good friend, a terrific adviser on boy problems, and a very supportive and generous person who I still can't believe I hooked up with via a classified apartment listing in the *Village Voice*. Someday I will pay her all that's in arrears. Dolsie Somah is the reason that there is occasionally a pathway to my bedroom amid all the mess; she's also, as far as I can tell, the most kind and virtuous person on earth. Thanks to Shirly Ip, Irina, and everyone at the Peter Coppola Salon for being as nice to me as they are to Stephanie Seymour, and for understanding that it is just as hard to write when your roots are growing out as it is to pose for the Victoria's Secret catalogue.

Thanks to John Lambrose for being such an apt household metaphor.

Thanks to Zap, the most excellent cat on earth, for being such good company.

Thanks to Beat Rodeo, Brendan, and everyone at the Ludlow Street Cafe for making Monday nights the best way to start the week.

Thanks to Amy Stein, Renata Miller, and everyone at the Writers' Room.

Thanks to Stephen Olson and Susan Litwack for being the first people to encourage me to write, and for making high school bearable. Thanks finally to Bruce Springsteen, Bob Dylan, Joni Mitchell, Lou Reed, and the other great inventors of words and music that made my adolescence, and my depression, somehow possible to survive.

◊

In memoriam: Richard Whitesell,
25 February 1962–13 June 1994.
Love never dies.

the greens and blues of the North Sea, the red pantile roofs. Then there was the dramatic setting of the lobster-claw harbour and the two opposing hills, one capped with a church and a ruined abbey, the other with Captain Cook's statue and the massive jawbone of a whale. I knew immediately that this was where the story had to take place, and that it began with a woman getting off a bus, feeling a little travel-sick, trying the place on for size.

When I heard that Macmillan planned to publish this novel in 2003, I toyed with the idea of rewriting it and updating it. After all, isn't it every writer's dream to get another chance years later at improving something one wrote in one's early days? But the more I thought about it, the more I realized that it just wouldn't work, that the world has changed so much since 1987, and that the events in *Caedmon's Song* couldn't happen in a world with mobile phones, e-mail, a McDonald's or Pizza Hut on every corner, and the current techniques of DNA testing. Genetic fingerprinting existed back then, as Joseph Wambaugh's *The Blooding* demonstrates very well, but it was still in its infancy. Besides, I was supposed to be leaving the police behind. Given the advances in forensic science since 1987, it seemed that if I were to update the book for 2003, it would be almost impossible to keep them in the background. Whitby has changed, too, especially the footpath along the top of the cliffs which plays such an important role in the book.

In the end, I settled for correcting a few minor points, changing a character's name, getting rid of an obtrusive comment about Margaret Thatcher. That sort of thing. In all other respects it's the original novel, now a period piece of sorts, a slice of late twentieth-century history, set in a time when you could smoke anywhere, get bed and breakfast for £9.50 a night and *Crocodile Dundee* was all the rage!

Ragûza 198, 200, 287
Râmi çiftliği 209
Revan 216
Rum 53, 57, 81, 82, 89, 94, 101, 102, 112, 114, 116, 159, 179, 216, 246, 257, 268, 294
Rumeli, Şarki/Doğu Rumeli 24, 27, 42, 49, 57, 61-63, 78, 94, 99, 105, 117, 118, 120, 138, 142, 145, 153, 155, 165, 167, 168, 174, 177, 179, 184, 193, 201, 208-210, 212, 213, 215, 216, 223, 224, 227, 228, 242, 250, 251, 255, 257, 260, 261, 263-266, 268, 270-273, 278, 284, 285, 288, 290, 293
Rus 1803 Fermanı 230
Rusya, Moskov Devleti 19, 20, 22, 23, 32, 41-43, 47, 48, 55-61, 64, 65, 74, 79, 82-86, 88, 90-96, 98-106, 108-127, 129, 131-133, 138, 144, 145, 147, 150, 152, 154-168, 170, 179, 180, 182, 183, 186-190, 196-198, 200-204, 210, 214-218, 222-231, 233-236, 238-240, 242-248, 250, 252, 255-257, 261-263, 266, 269, 270, 274-277, 279, 281, 284, 295, 297, 298, 300-302

Sadık Paşa 263
Saffet Paşa 249, 267
salgın 173, 175, 176
Sava Nehri 249
sayım, nüfus sayımı 44, 45, 133, 134, 136, 174, 179, 207-209, 225, 238, 299, 303
sevk 92, 93, 137, 158, 163, 167-169, 226, 243, 251, 252, 262, 264, 265, 275, 276, 284, 288, 301
sığınmacı(lar) 17-19, 26, 31-33, 51-53, 121, 222
Sırbistan 29, 43, 57, 137, 193, 210, 212, 225, 242, 250, 255, 264, 267, 274, 281
Sırp 42, 60, 108, 201, 203, 280, 281, 285-287, 290
Silistre 63, 70, 83, 89, 129, 130, 136, 137, 139, 140, 143, 145, 149, 152, 158, 168, 182, 210, 214, 232, 233, 241, 255
Silistre Muhacir Talimatnamesi, 1856 140
Silistre Talimatnamesi 63, 89, 129, 130, 136, 152, 210, 214, 241
Sivastopol 168, 232
Sofya 198, 255, 264, 265
Sohum 208, 257
Sokol 137
soy-sop 298, 302, 303
Suriye 17, 18, 31, 32, 51, 52, 70, 86, 97, 205, 212, 215, 222, 251, 252, 255, 266
Süleyman Paşa 263, 264

Şam 70, 72, 153, 205, 255
Şarki Rumeli Avrupa Komisyonu, 1878 142, 153
Şeyh Abdülkadir isyanı 222
Şeyh Mansur 239
Şeyh Şamil, - ayaklanması 186, 226, 227, 234, 239, 241-244
Şirket-i Hayriye, 1851 166, 167
Şumnu 209, 265

Tabiiyet kanunu, 1856 ve 1869 32, 83, 129, 136
Tanzimat 23, 25, 33, 39, 68, 69, 80-82, 84, 121, 125, 129-134, 137, 138, 141, 170, 172-174, 178, 184, 185, 190, 191, 297, 302, 303
Tanzimat Deklarasyonu, 1839 129, 172, 302, 303
Tapu Kanunu, 1847, 1859 130, 134
Tatar 24, 43, 44, 47, 50, 61, 103, 114, 118, 126, 151, 153, 159, 160, 179, 182, 198, 199, 201, 208, 210, 213-216, 227, 230, 232-234, 237, 251, 259, 265, 266
Tavattun Nizamnamesi, 1856 137
telgraf 23, 39, 164, 298, 300
Tercan 252
Tercüman (Prevodçik) gazetesi 201, 202
Tersane Konferansı/Anlaşması 94,

151, 227, 228, 235, 249-251, 259,
  261, 263, 265, 268, 302, 303
Tesalya 249
tezyid 142, 171, 207, 209-212, 228,
  248, 257, 259, 298, 300
Todleben, General 232
Trakya 28, 29, 125, 179, 180, 236,
  266, 271, 273, 289
transfer 47, 49, 62, 115, 138, 152, 154,
  158, 159, 161, 164, 165, 169, 175,
  186, 210, 215, 227, 232, 246, 247,
  250, 253, 264, 288
tren, demiryolları 39, 157, 159, 165,
  169, 170, 172, 178, 237, 288, 298,
  300
Tuna, - deltası 24, 94, 99, 114, 130,
  138, 139, 141, 144, 150, 153-161,
  164, 166, 167, 172, 173, 175, 178,
  179, 183, 188, 192, 209, 210, 214,
  226, 227, 229, 231, 233, 237, 239-
  243, 248, 255, 257, 263, 264, 301
Tunus 117, 154, 222
Türk, - uşağı 19, 20, 24, 25, 27-31, 33,
  36, 42, 45, 47, 49, 51, 57-62, 65,
  70, 81, 82, 85, 86, 92-95, 99, 106,
  117, 119, 128, 157, 162, 175, 181,
  182, 184, 185, 194, 196, 197, 199,
  208, 209, 212, 213, 221, 224, 227,
  228, 256, 258-260, 265-273, 275,
  278, 282, 293, 294, 296, 301-303

Türk Yurdu dergisi 202
Türkistan 222, 302
Türkiye 17, 18, 26, 30-32, 51-53, 60,
  156, 194, 205, 256

Umûm Muhacirîn Muhtelit
  Komisyonu 142

Van 147, 211, 217, 252
vapur, buharlı gemiler 122, 126,
  159, 164-168, 236, 247, 248,
  275, 298
vassal devletler 59, 221-223, 225
Vecihi Paşa, Muhacirin Komisyonu
  Reisi 170, 245

Xabze (Çerkes asabiyası) 239, 253

Yahudi 74, 81, 87, 100, 121, 122, 171,
  209, 212, 223, 228
yeniçeri(lik) 22, 69, 70, 131, 175, 180,
  181, 187, 221, 224, 302
Yenipazar Anlaşması (1879, Osmanlı-
  Habsburg) 282
yol hükmü 174
Yunan 39, 89, 92, 111, 215, 225, 249,
  257, 260, 261, 268, 293, 294, 296
Yunan Krallığı, Yunanistan 18, 43, 82,
  89, 111, 166, 168, 190, 215, 216,
  225, 228, 249, 260, 293-296

Zosia
(alt. Zosima)
Greek, meaning 'wisdom'. Actress Zosia Mamet is known for her roles in *Mad Men*, *Parenthood* and *Girls*.

Zoya
Greek, meaning 'life'. Zoya Kosmodemyanskaya is one of the former Soviet Union's most revered heroines, after fighting for the Russian rebellion during World War II.

Zula
African, meaning 'brilliant'.

Zuleika
Arabic, meaning 'fair and intelligent'. Also the name of Potiphar's wife in the Bible.

Zulma
Arabic, meaning 'peace'.

Zuzana
Hebrew, meaning 'lily'. More commonly used in the Czech and Slovak republics.

Zuzu
Czech, meaning 'flower'. The nickname for one of George Bailey's children in the film *It's A Wonderful Life*.

Names with positive meanings

Allegra – cheerful

Lucy – light

Augusta – magnificent

Phoebe – radiant

Felicia – lucky

Thalia – flourishing

Hilary – cheerful

Yoko – positive

is none—no sky, no horizon, only dazzling white—so he opens his door and leans out and looks for tire tracks: hanging from the steering wheel, leaning way down, his face a couple feet from the ground, hoping that nobody is driving toward him and doing likewise. Then, as the car slips off the road, he realizes that the track he is following is the track of his own left front tire heading into the deep ditch. The car eases down into the snow, and he squeezes out the window and climbs up onto the road. He is not too far from his neighbor's house. He can see it almost, and the woods. A massed army of corn stands in the snowy field. Visibility is not so bad as in the car, where his heavy breathing was fogging the glass. He's about a quarter-mile from home. The cigarettes, however, must be sitting on Wally's counter. They certainly aren't in the car. *A pretty dumb trip.* Town was a long way to go in a blizzard for the pleasure of coming back home. He could have driven his car straight to the ditch and saved everyone the worry. But what a lucky man. Some luck lies in not getting what you thought you wanted but getting what you have, which once you have it you may be smart enough to see is what you would have wanted had you known. He takes deep breaths and the cold air goes to his brain and makes him more sensible. He starts out on the short walk to the house where people love him and will be happy to see his face.

mouth, Dominica, April 10, 1915, with seven hundred and fifty barrels of sperm oil and the Valkyria came in a few days later with five hundred barrels, all of which was put aboard the R. W. Clark for transshipment to New Bedford. The Viola sailed for the western grounds under command of Captain Reed and arrived in New Bedford September 7, 1915, with nine hundred and eighty barrels of oil taken in the four months, thus ending a voyage of thirty-five months in the North and South Atlantic Ocean, having taken the large quantity of forty-seven hundred barrels of sperm oil during the voyage, which I believe has never been equaled by a vessel of the Viola's size, and lowering but three boats.

The Viola, having been to sea over five years on the two voyages, needed to be overhauled. It was necessary to remetal her bottom, replacing new copper and stripping off the old. It was too late when the repairs were finished to send her out that fall, so she was made fast at Pier 3, New Bedford, for the winter.

On April 21st, I again sailed in the Viola for a summer cruise in the North Atlantic Ocean, returning August 21st with five hundred and fifty barrels of sperm oil, thus completing my last voyage whaling. Having started in the business in May, 1879, now at the age of fifty-nine years and seven months I feel that the place I have filled can be and ought to be occupied by men younger in life. A feature of this last voyage was the taking of moving pictures of the whaling industry, which I hope may prove of interest to those who have read of, but have never seen, how the work is carried on at sea. The Viola sailed in September, 1917, commanded by Captain Joseph Lewis; returned to New Bedford July, 1918, with eleven hundred and fifty barrels of sperm oil and two hundred pounds ambergris. She sailed for another voyage September, 1918, with Captain Joseph Lewis, who had with him his wife and five-year-old daughter and a crew of twenty-four men. The vessel and crew were never reported or heard from again. Lost in the mysteries of the sea with all hands. Sad fate that has befallen so many that have pursued the going down to sea in ships.

THE END

INDEX

sprag 247
spragged 109
spreathed, spreethed 48
spuggy 274
squall 11, 22
squit 167
stagged 22
starve, starved,
    starving 105, **191**, 267
stay 339
steen 221
steimisher 280, **299**
stitching 196
stoater 318
stocious 294, 317
stoon 291, 303
stote, stoting, stoating,
    stoter, stoater 318, 333,
    339
stotty cake 275
stovies 339
stream the clome 22
stree 247
strides 156, 318, 339
strome 167
strushel 332
stythe 274
suckers 120–21, 140, **149**
swailing 22
sweating cobs 185
swingletrees,
    thribtrees 226–7, 247

tab **149**, 275
tacker 23
taflu 94
tag off 135, **149**
taid 98, 105, **109**
taigh beag 340
tairsgeir 329, 340
taitered **149**
tallboy 319
tarra **191**
tawch 109
t'awd man 204
teasy 12, 23

teddies 48
tenfoot, eightfoot 99, 205,
    217
tentless 339
teth 340
tha mi sgìth 340
tha naas 9
thee, tha, thysen,
    thysel 195, 211, 217
thee, thou 225
thole, thoil 217, 288, 303
thrashing 202, 217
thrawn 288, 303
threads 64
thribtrees 226–7
thriving 196
throstle **191**
through-other 303
throw money about like
    a man with no
    arms **149**
thutty 201
thwaite 195, 217
tidden 48
tiddy oggy *see* oggy
tidy 101, **109**
tigh 327, 340
till 235, 247, 282, 303
timdoodle 23
tippler toilet 176, **191**,
    316
tittamatorter 154, **167**
tittle-me-fancy **167**
titty-totty **167**
tittybabby **149**
to 48
tober 297, 304
Tocky 249
toon 261, 312
townie 183, **191**
tranklements 217
trenestatha 4
trepenner 222
trig 23
trim up 99, **109**
troshing 167

trun 243, **249**
trust my faith 74, **80**
tup 206, 218
twag, twagging 204, **218**
twirls 319
twitchbell 200
twitchel 38, 135, **149**
twitten 80
twp 109
tŷ bach 89, 96, **109**
tyke 218

uddent 48
uisge, uisge-beatha 309,
    340
un, um 48
up the stick **149**
urts 14, 23
us 210, 218

Valleys, the 109–10
vang 27
vean 23
veggs 36, 48
vennel 315, 333, **339**
verns 14, 23, 48
vex, vexed 73, 74, 80, 139,
    149, 183, 212
vitty, viddy 48
vuzz, vuzz-bush 23, **48**

wabbit 319, **339**
wabs 297
wack 249
wag it, play it, wack
    it 105, 179–80, **191**
wain 303, 318, **339**
wal 218
waldies 332
wannabe 80
wannum 48
want 14, 23
want-hill 23
wap 23
warm **149**
warped up 48

349

warspy 164
watter 149
way fore 48
wayzgoose 23
wean 318
weave your piece 192
wee 303–4
wee abearin 332
Welsh Not 83, 110
we'm 8
Wenglish 110
wesleybob 218
wet nelly 249
whack, bang, chin, smack 249
whang 218, 304
wheal 23

where's it to? 110
whoore 4
wick 203, 218
widel 23
winnard 11, 23
winnock 339
wipput 263
wir ain leid 309, 339
wish(t) 10, 23, 38, 48
withy 48
wob oer 149
wom 132, 149, 192
wor 266
wynd 314, 339

yachy da 90, 110
yaffle 164, 167

yam 218, 227, 247
yan, tan, tethera, methera, pimp, sethera, lethera, hovera, dovera, dik 201, 247–8
yat 192, 204, 205, 218, 248
yaws 36, 48
yed, yedache 173, 192
yek 221, 248
yellow noses 322
yer, year 110
yet up 36, 48
yock 298, 304
yorks 10
yous, yews 249
yowth 119–20, 149

Huskily he said, "No, Kamana. You were not wrong." Then, with a blossoming of joy, Ranulph drew her into his arms, and surrendered to his destiny.

And they all lived happily ever after.

ABOUT THE AUTHORS

Jo Beverley is the author of seventeen romance novels, all set in her native England. Her fiction has garnered many awards, including four Ritas, romance's top accolade, and a place on the *New York Times* bestseller list as part of the collection *Married at Midnight*. Jo lives in British Columbia, Canada, with her husband and sons, and once more has a garden to play with. Perhaps, if she plants the right flowers, the faeries will come

Karen Harbaugh has always loved fairy tales and myths and could never quite let go of them when she grew up. As a result, she became a writer and started making up her own, except she called them romance novels. In 1995, *Romantic Times* gave her their Reviewer's Choice Award for Best Fantasy Regency. Her most recent book is *Cupid's Mistake*, yet another myth disguised as a Regency romance. She lives in Washington State with her husband and son, and has, of course, a garden.

Barbara Samuel is a triple Rita Finalist and Janet Dailey award winner who has written five historical romances and several fantasy novellas under her own name. She has also written more than a dozen contemporary romances under the pseudonym Ruth Wind.

A *New York Times* list bestselling author, Mary Jo Putney has written nineteen novels and ten novellas. Her books have won numerous awards, including two Ritas, a *Romantic Times* Career Achievement Award, and the first Aphra Award for Book of the Year from the published authors chapter of the Romance Writers of America. Her most recent novel was *One Perfect Rose*. She lives in Maryland with her nearest and dearest, both two and four footed, and surrounds herself with as many flowers as she can persuade to grow.

INDEX

Windmills, 141, 142, 250.
Window tax, 203.
Windy Nook, 250.
Wingrove Avenue, 266; Cottage, 266; Gardens, 266; Hospital, 280; House, 266; Road, 266, 280; Terrace, 266.
Winlaton: pit, 56; Selby family, estate, 68; Crowley Ironworks, 91, 109-110, 231; in *1815*, 140; Reform Society, 171; forgemen in protest meeting against Peterloo, 172, 249; march of forgemen to Durham, *1831*, 174; Chartist pikes, 180; " Sacred Month," 180; elder Joseph Cowen, forgeman, 249.
Wintoun, Lord, 96, 97.
Wire ropes, coal haulage, 187.
Witton Park, 185, 188, 231.
Wood, Nicholas, 296, 308.
Woodside, 187.
Wool, export of, from Newcastle, 40, 43.
Wooler, 94, 96, 152.
Wooler, Jonathan, 171.
Woolsington, 314.
Woolworth's premises, Newcastle, 317.
Workhouse, 118, 208, 266, 279-280.
Workington, 107.
Workmen's trains, 235.
Worley St., 307.
Worswick, Rev. James, 157, 158.
Worswick St., 157, 269, 285.

Wouldhave, William, 143.
Wrestling, 222, 307.
Wyclif Baptist Church, 268.
Wylam: waggonways, 134; *Puffing Billy*, 136; pits, 140; ironworks closed down, 231; gift of Castle Hill to Royal Victoria Infirmary, 279; Nicholas Wood, 308.
Wyndham, Sir Charles, 51.

Yarmouth, 73, 89.
Yarnold, William, 200-201.
York, 2, 3; *Eburacum*, 7; chief town in Deira, 9; relieved by William I, *1069*, 14; Norman garrison destroyed, 14; liberty of Hexhamshire held by archbishop of, 18; legionary base for Roman Wall, 21; " county corporate," 31; seat of King's Council in the North, 46; surrender of liberties by archbishop, 47; St. Peter's, 47; in Pilgrimage of Grace, 48-49; execution of Earl of Northumberland, 50; Marquis of Newcastle besieged in, 75; Robert Trollop, 77; school clinic, 290.
York, House of, 27.
York and North Midland Rly., 191.
York, Newcastle and Berwick Rly, 191.
Young, Arthur, 104, 110, 113, 137.
Y.M.C.A., 268.

tossed it into the trash. He didn't need any mementos. He remembered that disaster only too well. He knew he would never forget it for the rest of his life.

He glanced back at Beth and Harry. They both looked tired. Beth stared into space, preoccupied with her own thoughts. But her face was serene; despite the hardships of their time underwater, Norman thought she looked almost beautiful.

"You know, Beth," he said, "you look lovely."

Beth did not seem to hear, but then she turned toward him slowly. "Why, thank you, Norman," she said.

And she smiled.

Look for these exciting novels
by *New York Times* bestselling author

MICHAEL CRICHTON

Available in bookstores everywhere.
Published by Ballantine Books.

Call toll free 1-800-733-3000 to order by phone and use your major credit card. Please mention interest code KAF-193K to expedite your order. Or use this coupon to order by mail.

__THE ANDROMEDA STRAIN	345-37848-2	$5.99
__CONGO	345-37849-0	$5.99
__EATERS OF THE DEAD	345-35461-3	$4.99
__JURASSIC PARK	345-37077-5	$6.99
__RISING SUN	345-38037-1	$6.99
__SPHERE	345-35314-5	$5.99
__THE TERMINAL MAN	345-35462-1	$5.99

Nonfiction:

__TRAVELS	345-37966-7	$10.00

Name_____
Address _____
City_____ State_____ Zip _____

Please send me the BALLANTINE BOOKS I have checked above.
I am enclosing $____
   plus
Postage & handling* $____
Sales tax (where applicable) $____
Total amount enclosed $____

*Add $2 for the first book and 50¢ for each additional book.

Send check or money order (no cash or CODs) to Ballantine Mail Sales, 400 Hahn Road, Westminster, MD 21157.

Prices and numbers subject to change without notice.
Valid in U.S. only
All order subject to availability.   KAF-193K

The night and the streets were ours and the future lay sparkling ahead.

And we thought we would know each other forever.

APACHES
Lorenzo Carcaterra

It is the early 1980s. Crack cocaine has made its devasting appearance. Violence is escalating and so is an unnerving lack of morality. Things are happening that have never happened before.

One of those things is the brutal kidnapping of an innocent twelve-year-old girl. But the kidnapper has made a deadly mistake. He has brought Boomer Frontieri back to life, back to the streets. And back into action. A New York City detective forced to retire after being wounded in a drug bust, Boomer thirsts to return to the life he loved – the life of a cop. When an old friend turns to him for help, Boomer has the excuse he needs. And when the simple kidnapping turns into something more, something much more evil, even more horrifying, Boomer realises that he can once again find a way to serve justice.

There are others like Boomer. Cops who can no longer be cops. He brings them together, bringing them back to life as well. Even as they face almost certain death. *Apaches* is the story of an extraordinary band of cops. Some might call them criminals. Some might call them heroes. But theirs is a world where good is always shadowed by bad, where right is almost indecipherable from wrong, and where the living can, within mere moments, cross over to the world of the dead.

"I så fall föreslår jag att du kommer hem till oss och käkar imorgon kväll."

"Imorgon är det tisdag."

"Ok, vi väntar till på fredag. Fast jag har en sak att bekänna också."

"Bekänna?"

"Ja. Jag har kommit över lite pengar."

"Va? Vad då för pengar."

"Inte så mycket, men jag vet inte riktigt om jag kan behålla dem."

"Gunnar, vad i hela friden dillar du om? Hur mycket är det frågan om?"

"Femtio euro."

"Du har... du har *kommit över* femtio euro? Hur då?"

Barbarotti suckade. "När jag satt utanför det där hotellet och låtsades vara tiggare..."

"Ja?"

"Det kom förbi en kvinna och gav mig femtio euro."

"Oj. Jag menar... du måste ha gjort ett gott intryck."

"Jo, eller sett väldigt lidande ut åtminstone. Men jag var ju liksom i tjänst. Är det korrekt att jag behåller dem?"

Eva Backman funderade några sekunder. "Knivigt", sa hon. "Men vet du, Gunnar, jag tycker du ska köpa ett riktigt gott vin till på fredag, och så håller vi tyst om saken."

"Så har vi det på vårt samvete båda två?"

"Precis. Partners in crime... nej, du kan inte kyssas och köra bil samtidigt."

"Så hur var Nya Zeeland?"

Mahler justerade pjäserna och tände sin cigarr.

"Inte så dumt", svarade Van Veeteren. "Men nu pratar vi om någonting annat."

"Jaså minsann. Vad då, till exempel?"

"Förslagsvis den här", sa Van Veeteren och strök försiktigt med fingrarna över den tunna boken som låg på bordet bredvid schackbrädet. "Det kom som en överraskning, du nämnde ingenting om det senast vi sågs."

"Glömde väl bort det", sa Mahler.

"Man kan väl för fan inte glömma bort en diktsamling man just skickat till trycket?" sa Van Veeteren. "Även om det är ens tolfte."

"Trettonde", sa Mahler. "Det är ju bara ord, för övrigt."

"Inte så bara."

"Kanske det. Nej, det är nog det sista som lämnar oss. När kroppen har fallit i bitar så ligger vi väl där och lyssnar till surret i skallen innan ridån går ner... eller vad tror du?"

"Vad skulle vi annars göra?" sa Van Veeteren. "Varför heter den som den gör?"

"*En skiva bröd och andra dikter*", sa Mahler och blåste ut ett tankfullt rökmoln. "Tänkte först kalla den *En korvskiva och andra dikter*, men då stöter man bort vegetarianerna."

"Det förklarar saken", sa Van Veeteren. "Ja, man måste förstås tänka på sina läsare."

"Alltid", instämde Mahler. "Ditt drag, min vän."

Van Veeteren grubblade en stund. Sedan flyttade han fram en bonde.

"Ser man på", sa Mahler. "En nyhet."

"Kallar du e2–e4 för en nyhet?" undrade Van Veeteren.

"Nej. Men du flyttade med vänster hand. Det brukar du aldrig göra."

"En ren tillfällighet", sa Van Veeteren. "Varsågod, poetens drag."

drain had left no degrading marks upon me; and I think the real reason for that was that I had never truly belonged there.

During these first weeks of freedom I would not only have to find some way of earning my living but also look after poor Picolino and keep him too. It was a serious responsibility that I had taken upon myself. Yet although he would be a heavy burden I'd keep my promise to the governor and I'd never leave the poor fellow until I'd managed to get him into a hospital, where he would be cared for by people who knew what they were about.

Should I tell my father that I was free? He'd not heard from me for years. In any case where was he? The only news of me he'd had was the visits of the gendarmes whenever I made a break. No, I mustn't be in too much of a hurry. I had no right to open a wound that had perhaps been almost healed by the passing of the years. I'd write when I was really on my feet, when I had a solid and straightforward, though perhaps modest job, so that I'd be able to say, 'Dear Papa, your little boy is free and he has become an honest man – he has gone straight. He lives in such-and-such a way and he has such-and-such a position. You no longer have to hang your head when he is mentioned, and that is why I am writing to tell you that I always have loved and honoured you and always will.'

This was war-time: who could tell whether the Germans were there in my little village? The Ardèche was not a very important part of France. It wouldn't be completely occupied. What could they find there, apart from the chestnuts? Yes, it was only when I was properly established and worthy of it that I'd write home, or rather try to write.

Where should I go now? I'd settle in a village called La Callao, by the goldmines. There I'd live the year I was required to spend in the country. What should I do? God knows. Cross those bridges when you come to them. If you have to dig to earn your bread, why then you'll just dig and that's all there is to it. To begin with I've got to learn how to live as a free man. It won't be easy. Apart from these few months in Georgetown, I'd not had to worry about earning my daily bread for the last thirteen years. Still, at Georgetown I'd not done so badly. The adventure would go on, and it was up to me to find ways of earning my living – without doing anyone any harm, of course. I'd see. So tomorrow it would be La Callao.

Seven o'clock in the morning. A splendid tropical sun, a

cloudless blue sky, birds singing their delight in life, my friends gathered at the garden gate. Picolino, newly shaved and cleanly dressed in civilian clothes. There was an officer there waiting with my friends, and he was going with us as far as the village of El Dorado.

'Embrace us,' said Toto, 'and then just go. That'll be best for everyone.'

'Good-bye, brothers. If ever you pass by Le Callao, look me up. If I have a place of my own, it'll be yours.'

'Good-bye, Papi. Good luck!'

Quickly we went down to the landing stage and got into the boat. Picolino walked very well: it was only above the waist that he was paralysed – his legs were quite all right. In under a quarter of an hour we were on the other side of the river.

'Right: here are Picolino's papers. Good luck, you two. From this moment on you're free. Adios!'

It's as easy as that to drop the chains you've been dragging for thirteen years. 'From this moment on you're free.' They turn their backs, which means that nobody is keeping watch on you any more. And that's all. In a few minutes we had climbed the cobbled path from the river. All we had was a little bundle with three shirts in it and a spare pair of trousers. I was wearing my navy-blue suit, a white shirt and a blue tie to match.

But as you may imagine, making a new life for oneself is not quite as easy as sewing on a button. And although today, twenty-five years later, I am a married man with a daughter of my own, a Venezuelan citizen living happily in Caracas, I only got there after a great many other adventures, some of them successful and others disastrous, but all of them the adventures of a free man and an upright citizen. Maybe one day I'll tell them, together with a good many other remarkable stories that I didn't have room for here.

WENJ—servant at an inn along the coast road in Tysan that borders the Korias flats.
 pronounced: wenge
 root meaning: *wenje*—beetle
WERPOINT—fishing town and outpost on the northeast coast of Fallowmere, Rathain. Musterpoint for Lysaer's war host.
 pronounced: were-point
 root meaning: *wyr*—all/sum
WEST GATE PROPHECY—prophecy made by Dakar the Mad Prophet in Third Age 5061, which forecast the return of royal talent through the West Gate, and the bane of Desh-thiere and a return to untrammeled sunlight.
WESTCLIFF—port city located on the coast of Carithwyr, Kingdom of Havish.
WESTFEN—fishing town on the coast of Deshir, Kingdom of Rathain.
WESTWOOD—forest located in Camris, Tysan, north of the Great West Road.
WORLDSEND GATES—set at the four compass points of the continent of Paravia. These were spelled portals constructed by the Fellowship of Seven at the dawn of the Third Age, and were done in connection with the obligations created by their compact with the Paravian races which allowed men to settle on Athera.

Magician
Raymond E. Feist
New Revised Edition

Raymond E. Feist has prepared a new, revised edition, to incorporate over 15,000 words of text omitted from previous editions so that, in his own words, 'it is essentially the book I would have written had I the skills I possess today'.

At Crydee, a frontier outpost in the tranquil Kingdom of the Isles, an orphan boy, Pug is apprenticed to a master magician – and the destinies of two worlds are changed forever. Suddenly the peace of the Kingdom is destroyed as mysterious alien invaders swarm through the land. Pug is swept up into the conflict but for him and his warrior friend, Tomas, an odyssey into the unknown has only just begun. Tomas will inherit a legacy of savage power from an ancient civilisation. Pug's destiny is to lead him through a rift in the fabric of space and time to the mastery of the unimaginable powers of a strange new magic...

'Epic scope... fast-moving action... vivid imagination'
Washington Post

'Tons of intrigue and action'
Publishers Weekly

ISBN 0 586 21783 3

against him and letting her cling to him till her equilibrium was restored.

As soon as she could, she repeated her question. 'Darling, what does it mean?'

'Exactly what it says, I hope. That's why I couldn't answer it before. But now, if all goes as planned and you agree, I can post it before we leave Wales tomorrow.'

She was still stunned and incredulous. She couldn't take it in, and looked in puzzled fashion up to him for explanation.

'Darling Fran, I'm telling you the truth! Do you think I would play silly jokes on you about *that*? Of all things in the world, the thing I want most? I asked you not to be cross with me, because I honestly have had no other choice.'

'Tell me,' she said.

He breathed a great sigh, pulled her head on to his shoulder, and began. 'I can hardly believe it, either. In the first batch of letters Greg sent on to me, there was a letter from my solicitor informing me that he was investigating a rumour from the USA of an accident in Spain involving Janice. He had tried to ring me at home, but of course had been told I was away and that letters were being forwarded.

'I rang my solicitor. You were very helpful, sweetheart, not wanting to accompany me to the telephone in the daytime! He had been in touch with hers in New York, from whom he had heard that she and her sugar-daddy had been in Granada on holiday when the old man had slipped down the steps of a swimming pool and had had to be taken to hospital, seriously injured. His "wife", who had held him up in the water till help arrived, was suffering from shock herself. Two days later, when I rang him again, he had just heard that Mr Joseph's wife had died suddenly, apparently from an overstrained heart. I simply dared not believe it, but in any case I had no proof that Mr Joseph's dead "wife" was Janice. So they set to work. There was utter confusion – but in the end her passport disclosed that the dead lady was a British citizen: Janice Aurelia Denton, previously Burbage, maiden name Denton.'

William was incapable of sitting still another second. He sprang to his feet, seeming to Fran two inches taller than usual, and flung his arms wide as if getting rid of a load carried long on his shoulders.

'Darling, it had to be her! But I still had to have proof of her death. It could have been misreported. If it was true, then, like Winston Churchill crossing the South African border, I could shout, "I'm William bloody Burbage, and I'm free."'

'God, but it has been difficult! Confirmation came the day before yesterday. As I was her legal husband, the death certificate had to be released to me, and I asked for it to be sent straight to the registrar in Builth. I picked it up yesterday. The poor old man has now died, too, so there is bound to be a lot of international to-ing and fro-ing, but as far as any of my advisers can see, they needn't involve me. Do you feel strong enough to come up and watch the sunset with me now? Because I'm afraid there are a couple of questions only you can answer.'

She hadn't really taken any of it in, yet. The significance of it all, especially to him . . . She looked up at him, and read in his face such a power of emotion that it awed her into stillness. They stood facing each other, simply holding hands. The circuit was complete and the current running through it lit up the whole world.

'Quick,' he said, 'or we shall miss the sunset.'

They scrambled up, and faced the splendour of the west, lovelier, they thought, than ever.

'Before the sun touches down, will you answer my questions?' he asked.

'If I can,' she said.

'Then – will you marry me?'

She couldn't answer. Words simply would not come. Instead she turned towards him, and held up her face to be kissed. She was not at all surprised to find his face as wet as her own.

'So what more is there to ask?' she said.

'Can you prove you are as free to marry me at Rhulen Church tomorrow morning as I can that I'm free to marry you? I've got it all set up with Nigel. He'll take your word for it, and accept the evidence afterwards, but I want it to be complete, final, from tomorrow for ever and for ever.'

Her mind raced. Brian's death certificate had been in her bank for more than twenty-five years. But – she opened her handbag, fumbling for the zip-fastener that closed an inside pocket. She never undid or sorted out except in emergency the slim little plastic wallet inside that held her driving licence and such things, even though she transferred it day-by-day from one bag to another. There it still was! The cover of the last war-widow's pension book she had ever used, having had her pension paid directly into a special account at her bank from the time she had ceased to be Brian's widow in anything but name and law.

He heaved a great sigh of satisfaction, and put it into his breast pocket.

'Watch the sun go down on your last day as Frances Catherwood,' he said. 'When it goes down tomorrow, you'll be Frances Burbage. My wife. *My very own legal wife.*'

'And we are going home,' she answered, cuddling up to him, while the sun slid behind the distant hill.

He swept her into his arms and said gloatingly, 'So we are, to spend our honeymoon, as I always told you we should, at Benedict's.'

MARRIED EXCLAMATION WE WILL BE DOWN ON A DELAYED HONEYMOON AS SOON AS POSSIBLE BUT EUROPE IS GOING TO BE HOME STOP LOVE TO ALL AND FROM RAIN TOO STOP JUSTINE

Meggie put the form down on the table and stared wide-eyed through the window at the wealth of autumn roses in the garden. Perfume of roses, bees or roses. And the hibiscus, the bottlebrush, the ghost gums, the bougainvillaea up above the world so high, the pepper trees. How beautiful the garden was, how alive. To see its small things grow big, change, and wither; and new little things come again in the same endless, unceasing cycle.

Time for Drogheda to stop. Yes, more than time. Let the cycle renew itself with unknown people. I did it all to myself, I have no one else to blame. And I cannot regret one single moment of it.

The bird with the thorn in its breast, it follows an immutable law; it is driven by it knows not what to impale itself, and die singing. At the very instant the thorn enters there is no awareness in it of the dying to come; it simply sings and sings until there is not the life left to utter another note. But we, when we put the thorns in our breasts, we know. We understand. And still we do it. Still we do it.

All Futura Books are available at your bookshop or newsagent, or can be ordered from the following address:
Futura Books, Cash Sales Department,
P.O. Box 11, Falmouth, Cornwall.

Please send cheque or postal order (no currency), and allow 45p for postage and packing for the first book plus 20p for the second book and 14p for each additional book ordered up to a maximum charge of £1.63 in U.K.

Customers in Eire and B.F.P.O. please allow 45p for the first book, 20p for the second book plus 14p per copy for the next 7 books, thereafter 8p per book.

Overseas customers please allow 75p for postage and packing for the first book and 21p per copy for each additional book.

We were about to pass the Four Turnings entrance. I leant forwards to the driver: 'Stop here, please,' I said. 'Stop here for a moment.'

I climbed out, and ran towards the gates: the light was like diamonds and the air smelt of the future. My heart was beating fast, and my hands were shaking. The sea is inaudible from there, but that morning I could hear it. Had I made the right choice, or the wrong one? I had made a *beginning*, I decided — and to begin felt perilous and joyful. For the first time in my life, I was answerable to no one. I was neither daughter nor wife; from now on, for better or worse, I alone would determine my future.

Beside me, Barker made a low whining sound; I felt the soft fur rise on his neck. I bent to reassure him, and then, as I straightened up, I saw — I'm almost sure I saw — someone moving through the trees towards me. She was very swift; I glimpsed only a passing brightness, a quick glitter of movement — but I felt the burn of her glance and it gave me courage.

I think a final salutation passed between us — I certainly felt it did, though I might have imagined it. I waited. When the air was ordinary again, I returned to the car, and told the driver to take me to the station.

from the east, only made him all the more certain they had been on a fool's errand, attempting to drive across the mountains, to seize a city reported to be abandoned. He had briefly wondered at the sanity of the demon, but given what had happened since, he said a prayer each night to Kalkin, thanking the god of gamblers for blessing him. How he had survived when so many others had been destroyed by the Emerald Queen or the demon was beyond him.

But now he had more immediate needs. His army was a long way from home and hungry. The good news was that as he traveled north the lands were more abundant, and his men were starting to eat well again. He said to Kahil, 'Word is to be sent south that any of those who managed to get away from Darkmoor could come to Ylith, to winter there.'

'Very well, General,' said the intelligence officer, who saluted and left the tent.

Fadawah also knew the Saaur were out there somewhere, and he was concerned. If he could speak to Jatuk he might convince the leader of the lizard people that he was also a dupe, a tool used and almost discarded, but if he failed that, the angry lizard would seek someone upon whom to vent his rage. As the highest remaining officer of the Emerald Queen's Army, Fadawah was a logical choice.

Fadawah sat back on the small stool in his tent. He had been cast upon a distant shore by a capricious fate, but it was his nature to turn an advantage wherever he might. That was why he had become the most successful general in Novindus, rising from mercenary captain in the Eastlands, to Military Overlord of the Emerald Queen.

His senior captain, Nordan, said, 'What will we do once we've taken this Ylith, General?'

Fadawah said, 'We've paid in blood for other people's greed and ambition, my old friend.' He leaned forward, putting his elbows on his knees. 'Now we serve our own.'

He smiled at his old companion. His thin face looked especially sinister in the faint light from the small lantern that hung from the tent pole. 'How would you like to be General of our armies?'

Nordan said, 'But if I become General, what about you?'

Fadawah said, 'I become King.'

His finger outlined the coast between Krondor and Ylith. 'The Kingdom's Western Capital is in ruins, and no law exists between it and Ylith.' He considered his options. 'Yes, King of the Bitter Sea. How does that sound?'

Nordan bowed. 'It sounds ... appropriate, Your Majesty.'

Fadawah laughed as the cool fall wind blew outside the tent.

Reading Group Questions

1) Cold War Berlin is crucial to the plot of the novel, and can be read almost as a character in itself. How does the unique location influence the actions of the characters? Could Thomas and Petra have lived happily ever after in another city?

2) Thomas is unable to truly move forward with his life, as he is haunted by his memories of Petra. What role does memory play in the novel?

3) How does Thomas's relationship with his parents affect his interactions with Petra and other characters in the novel?

4) What does Thomas learn from his trips into East Berlin, and how does this change his perception of life on the other side of the Wall?

5) There are two sides to every story: how do Petra's notebooks alter your interpretation of the novel and your response to its characters?

6) The many deceptions in the novel show the distrust and paranoia that permeates every element of a police state. What does the novel tell you about the importance of trust? Could Petra have told the truth?

7) Thomas is filled with guilt and shame when he reads Petra's notebooks. Is he entirely to blame for the dramatic conclusion of the central relationship?

8) What do you see as Alastair's role in the novel? How did you respond to him, and how does he help your understanding of the other characters and the city of Berlin?

9) It is better to have loved and lost . . . Do you agree with this, or do you think it is just more painful?

10) 'Are we ever truly free of the moment?' What does Thomas means by this and what do you think is the truth?

Douglas Kennedy's previous novels include the critically acclaimed bestsellers *The Big Picture*, *The Pursuit of Happiness*, *A Special Relationship* and *The Woman in the Fifth*. He is also the author of three highly praised travel books. His work has been translated into twenty-two languages. In 2006 he was awarded the French decoration of Chevalier de l'Ordre des Arts et des Lettres. Born in Manhattan, he has two children and currently divides his time between London, Paris, Berlin and Maine.

For more information please visit www.douglaskennedynovelist.com. Become a fan at www.facebook.com/DouglasKennedyBooks

ALSO BY DOUGLAS KENNEDY

Fiction
The Dead Heart
The Big Picture
The Job
The Pursuit of Happiness
A Special Relationship
State of the Union
Temptation
The Woman in the Fifth
Leaving the World

Non-fiction
Beyond the Pyramids
In God's Country
Chasing Mammon

Mission Services.

Hymn 778.   Hymn of Eve.—9 9 9 8. 8 8 8 8.   T. A. Arne, 1710–1788.

A - men.

"I will go in the strength of the Lord God."

f   I WILL go in the strength of the LORD
    In the path He hath mark'd for my feet:
I will follow the light of His word,
    Nor shrink from the dangers I meet.
His presence my steps shall attend;
    His fulness my wants shall supply;
On Him, till my journey shall end,
    My hope shall securely rely.

I will go in the strength of the LORD
    To the work He appoints me to do;
In the joy which His smile shall afford
    My soul shall her vigour renew.
His wisdom will guard me from harm,
    His pow'r my sufficiency prove;
I will trust His omnipotent arm,
    I will rest in His covenant love.

I will go in the strength of the LORD
    To each conflict which faith may require;
His grace, as my shield and reward,
    My courage and zeal shall inspire.
If He issue the word of command
    To meet and encounter the foe,
Though with sling and with stone in my hand,
    In the strength of the LORD I will go.

                                                     E. Turney.

Mission Services.

Hymn 779. GAUDIUM CÆLESTE.—5 5.7 7.7 7.6. Sir H. PARRY.

[Copyright 1904 by the Proprietors of Hymns Ancient and Modern.]

"There is joy in the presence of the angels of God over one sinner that repenteth."

  f THERE was joy in heav'n,
        There was joy in heav'n,
When this goodly world to frame
The LORD of might and mercy came;
Shouts of joy were heard on high,
And the stars sang from the sky,
    Glory to GOD in heav'n.

  f There was joy in heav'n,
      There was joy in heav'n,
When the billows heaving dark,
Sank around the stranded ark,
dim And the rainbow's watery span
Spake of mercy, hope to man,
 p   And peace with GOD in heav'n.

  f There was joy in heav'n,
      There was joy in heav'n,
p When of love the midnight beam
Dawn'd on the towers of Bethlehem,
cr And along the echoing hill
Angels sang "On earth good will,
f   And glory in the heav'n!"

  f There is joy in heav'n,
      There is joy in heav'n,
mf When the soul that went astray
Turns to CHRIST, the living Way,
And, by grace of heav'n subdued,
Breathes a prayer of gratitude;
 f Oh, there is joy in heav'n.

Bishop HEBER, 1827.

11

Oh! Friends no more! They are – what name for those? –
        Friends' phantom-flight
Knocking at my heart's window-pane at night,
Gazing on me, that speaks 'We were' and goes –
Oh, withered words, once fragrant as the rose!

12

Pinings of youth that might not understand!
        For which I pined,
Which I deemed changed with me, kin of my kind:
But they grew old, and thus were doomed and banned:
None but new kith are native of my land!

13

Midday of life! My second youth's delight!
        My summer's park!
Unrestful joy to long, to lurk, to hark!
I peer for friends! – am ready day and night,
For my new friends. Come! Come! The time is right!

* * *

14

This song is done – the sweet sad cry of rue
        Sang out its end;
A wizard wrought it, he the timely friend,
The midday-friend – no, do not ask me who;
At midday 'twas, when one became as two.

15

We keep our Feast of Feasts, sure of our bourne,
        Our aims self-same:
The Guest of Guests, friend Zarathustra, came!
The world now laughs, the grisly veil was torn,
And Light and Dark were one that wedding-morn.

FROM THE SANSKRIT

11

Of friends no need. They say, "what name for those, a
Friend, jealous ofttimes-slight,
Knocking at my heart's window-pane at night.
Calling on me, that ghosts? 'No; wine,' and gold
Oh, withered weeds, more fragrant in the mind.

12

Blooms of youth that might not understand
For wish I pined,
Which I deemed charged with me, kin of my kind;
But they grew old, and thus were doomed and burned
More our new lods are native as my land.

13

Maiden of fire! My second youth's delight,
My summer's park;
Un-aerial joy, ardent, to lark, to hark!
I peer for friends — see ready day and night,
For my new friends, "Come! Come! The time is right!

* * *

14

This song is done — the notes are dry of juice
Sing on in cud.
A second sanctuperit, let the thirsty feared,
The middle friend — no, do! not ask me why;
Af widely 'twas, when one became as two.

15

We keep our Feast of Feasts, we, at our change,
Our own self-same.
The Guest of Guests, bread Cranberries Come
The world, now laughs, the girlf, red was fair
And I, lyre and Duet were one this wedding-morn.

those leeks again. The vegetables concerned might even be able to walk there on their own.

Spying a young girl holding a big basket of snowdrops and sweet peas, Angus reined in his horse and hailed her. "How much?" he asked her as she came running toward him.

"A copper a bunch."

"No. For the lot."

Her eyes widened. Angus guessed she was younger than Cassy but a bit older than Beth. A pretty lass. But not as pretty as his girls. His request had sent her into a confusion of risky mental calculations and uncertainty, so he solved it by handing her a gold piece. "Tie the basket to the saddle bags with some fancy ribbon and we'll call it done."

She had the sense not to argue. Her hands, he noticed, were rough and callused, the skin toughened by farm work. "What's your name?" he asked when she'd finished securing the basket.

"Bronnie."

"Split the gold piece before you go home, Bronnie," he told her. "Take half home to your Da, and buy yourself some fancies with the rest. No one but me and you need ever know the price you got for the basket." He rode away, knowing from the worry in her face that she wouldn't do it.

Shrugging gently, Angus kicked the bay into motion. Home. He could smell it, he was quite sure of that. Smell rabbit in Darra's cook pot, and some sticky honey monstrosity cooked up by Beth on the hearth. Gods, but you knew a man was a fool and in love when he ate his women's burned cooking!

He couldn't get there soon enough. Caution demanded that he work his way around the oldgrowths and the stream, but caution could go to the nine spiraling hells. He'd been cautious for too long. It was time to get to his family by the quickest, shortest route.

Some of the flowers were lost in the gallop and he grinned,

imagining the trail he left. Some poor fool might follow it, believing there must be a princess at the end of such a scattering of blooms. He'd get an ugly middle-aged bordeman instead. Angus slapped his thigh. He hoped there wouldn't be kissing.

His grin fell a bit as he left the main path and took the little horse-trail that led to the Lok farm. No smoke. Darra must be cleaning out the hearth. A shiver of anxiety passed down through his shoulders into his spine. This trail hadn't been walked on for months. The grass was thick and untrodden. And the apple trees in the east orchard—they hadn't been cut back since before winter. Darra usually tended them like babies.

Angus Lok's mouth went dry.

As the trail wound around a low mound of blackberry bushes, he caught his first sight of the house. Burned. The walls were black and the roof had partially collapsed. Even before the horror of it hit him, there was a part of his brain that took in the details. This had not been recently done. There was no odor of char in the air, and the blackening on the walls had been crazily streaked by many rains.

"They got away," he said out loud, hardly knowing that he did it. "They must have got away."

But he'd been a member of the Phage too long to fool himself with false hope. For twenty years he'd been trained for the worst.

And now it was finally here.

The Sull horse knew, he *knew*, and he slowed to let his rider dismount. Angus's feet touched earth, and he made a bargain with his gods. "Take me now," he murmured. "Bring them back and take me instead."

The gods didn't answer. The gods were dead.

Angus took a breath to steady himself, and then walked into his house.

4. (p. 646) *The pievano.* 'Parish priest'. (GE)

Chapter 69
1. (p. 650) There is no division into a separate chapter in the MS.

Chapter 70
1. (p. 654) *Black Brethren ... white under his black.* Augustinian friars wear a black habit and cape; Dominicans, a white tunic and scapular, covered by a black cloak and hood.
2. (p. 654) *backslided into false hair.* Earlier editions read here: 'Monna Brigida, who had retrograded to false hair ...'

Chapter 71
1. (p. 665) *a necessary condition of his life.* A deleted passage in the MS reads here: 'Neither was that part of his confession quite unforeshadowed for Romola, in which he declared that he had begun to preach the coming scourge & renovation without the suggestion of visions or any supernatural teaching, but solely from a conviction founded on arguments, drawn from Scripture & reason, & that finding his doctrine lay hold on men's minds, he sought to tighten its grasp by affirming still higher evidence than he possessed. Romola's habitual contact with minds sarcastically critical of the Frate made her keenly sensitive to whatever seemed to justify their criticism. She had again & again felt uneasy, when he was preaching, at the perception that he was being urged into impromptu statements, & even when he narrated his great vision of the Divine sword hanging from the sky, which she did not doubt to have been originally a vision, she had always felt inclined to shut her ears when he went on amplifying it by an elaborate accompaniment of articulate voices.'

This was evidently deleted as being too critical of Savonarola at a point in the story at which our, and Romola's sympathy for him is required.
2. (p. 665) *change of external conditions.* A deleted passage in the MS reads here: 'Romola remembered how she herself had been subject to continual fluctuations in surveying her own impulses & conduct in the years she had lived through with Tito. Often if some one had condemned her, that condemnation would have turned the scale, & and she would have said, "I was driven more by pride & anger than by anything better".'
3. (p. 666) *But therefore ... to all time.* This sentence was not italicized in any earlier edition.

Chapter 72
1. (p. 668) *now, at the first sight of the horrible implements.* In earlier editions this reads: 'and now, at the first threat and first sight of the horrible implements ...'

2. (p. 669) *the Tetto de' Pisani*. In all editions of the novel George Eliot has 'Tetta de' Pisani' at this point, though she spells the name of the building correctly in Chapter 65. '*Tetta*' unfortunately means 'a breast' or 'teat'; '*tetto*' 'a roof'. I have corrected the mistake.
3. (p. 670) *Jacopo Nardi*. Jacopo Nardi (1476–1563) had been a disciple of Savonarola's, and had held various offices under the Florentine Republic. In 1527 he was instrumental in defeating Medicean troops attacking the Palazzo della Signoria. When the Medici finally suppressed the Republic in 1530, Nardi took refuge in Venice. His major literary work, the *Istorie della Città di Firenze*, which covers the years 1494 to 1532, was published posthumously in 1582.

George Eliot read Nardi's *History* in October 1861, and drew extensively on it for her own account of Florence in the period.
4. (p. 670) *cut off from the Church Militant*. The bishop, in degrading Savonarola, uttered the words '*Separo te ab Ecclesia militante atque triumphante*' – 'I cut you off from the Church militant and triumphant.' Savonarola is said to have calmly replied, '*Militante, non triumphante; hoc enim tuum non est*' – 'From the Church militant, but not the Church triumphant; that you cannot do.'

EPILOGUE

1. (p. 674) '*Spirito gentil*'. The opening words of Petrarch's *canzone* (numbered LIII in most editions of the *Rime*):

> 'Spirito gentil che quelle membra reggi
> dentro a le qua' peregrinando alberga
> un signor valoroso, accorto e saggio …'

'Noble spirit, ruling those limbs within which, on his pilgrimage (of life), lives a man who is valiant, clear-sighted and wise.'

This *canzone* is addressed to a statesman to whom Petrarch looks for the future resurgence of Rome and Italy. It is highly appropriate that Lillo should be reading this particular poem, for it leads into the subsequent discussion of true greatness. The poem would also have been taken by many Victorian readers as prophetic of the leaders of the *Risorgimento*.
2. (p. 675) *he never thought of anything cruel or base*. In earlier editions this sentence reads: 'I believe, when I first knew him, he never thought of doing anything cruel or base.'
3. (p. 675) *Yet calamity overtook him*. The MS reads here: 'Yet calamity came upon him.' The present sentence, with its different emphasis, was introduced into the *Cornhill* text.

The man on the throne trembled. His lips drew back in a rictus snarl. 'I shall break you. Each of you. I swear this upon the bones of twelve million sacrifices. K'rul, you shall fade from the world, you shall be forgotten. Draconus, what you create shall be turned upon you. And as for you, woman, unhuman hands shall tear your body into pieces, upon a field of battle, yet you shall know no respite – thus, my curse upon you, Sister of Cold Nights. Kallor Eiderann Tes'thesula, one voice, has spoken three curses. Thus.'

They left Kallor upon his throne, upon its heap of bones. They merged their power to draw chains around a continent of slaughter, then pulled it into a warren created for that sole purpose, leaving the land itself bared. To heal.

The effort left K'rul broken, bearing wounds he knew he would carry for all his existence. More, he could already feel the twilight of his worship, the blight of Kallor's curse. To his surprise, the loss pained him less than he would have imagined.

The three stood at the portal of the nascent, eternally lifeless realm, and looked upon their handiwork.

Then Draconus spoke. 'I am forging a sword.'

K'rul and the Sister of Cold Nights nodded, for this was known to them both.

'The power I have invested possesses a . . . a finality.'

'Then,' K'rul whispered, 'you must make alterations in the final shaping.'

'So it seems. I shall need to think long on this.'

After a long moment, K'rul and his brother turned to their sister.

She shrugged. 'I shall endeavour to guard myself. When my destruction comes, it will be through betrayal and naught else. There can be no precaution against such a thing, lest my life become its own nightmare of suspicion and mistrust. To this, I shall not surrender. Until that moment, I shall continue to play the mortal game.'

'Careful, then,' K'rul murmured, 'whom you choose to fight for.'

'Find a companion,' Draconus advised. 'A worthy one.'

'Wise words from you both. I thank you.'

There was nothing more to be said. The three had come

together, with an intent they had now achieved. Perhaps not in the manner they would have wished, but it was done. And the price had been paid. Willingly. Three lives and one, each destroyed. For the one, the beginning of eternal hatred. For the three, a fair exchange.

Elder Gods, it has been said, embodied a host of unpleasantries.

In the distance, the beast watched the three figures part ways. Riven with pain, white fur stained and dripping blood, the gouged pit of its lost eye glittering wet, it held its hulking mass on trembling legs. It longed for death, but death would not come. It longed for vengeance, but those who had wounded it were dead. There but remained the man seated on the throne, the one who had laid waste to the beast's home. Time enough for the settling of that score.

A final longing filled the creature's ravaged soul. Somewhere, amidst the conflagration of the Fall and the chaos that followed, it had lost its mate and was now alone. Perhaps she still lived. Perhaps she wandered, wounded as he was, searching the broken wastes for a sign of him. Or, perhaps she had fled, in pain and terror, to the warren that had given fire to her spirit. Wherever she had gone – assuming she still lived – he would find her.

The three distant figures unveiled warrens, each vanishing into their Elder realms. The beast elected to follow none of them. They were young entities as far as he and his mate were concerned, and the warren she might have fled to was, in comparison to those of the Elder Gods, ancient. The path that awaited him was perilous, and he knew fear in his labouring heart. The portal that opened before him revealed a grey-streaked, swirling storm of power. The beast hesitated, then strode into it.

And was gone.

the steps. Richard hugged the furry beast, and Gratch enfolded him in arms and wings. Each stroked the other's back, and each grinned in his own way.

When they finally sat up, Gratch hunched down, staring curiously at Richard's face. With the back of a huge claw, he stroked Richard's jaw.

Richard felt his smooth face as he smiled. 'It's gone. I'm not going to have a beard anymore.'

Gratch's nose wrinkled in disgust. He let out a gurgling growl of displeasure.

Richard laughed. 'You'll get used to it.' They sat together in the quiet of the dawn. 'Do you know, Gratch, that I'm a wizard?'

Gratch gurgled a laugh and frowned dubiously. Richard wondered how a gar could know what a wizard was. Gratch never failed to astonish him with what he knew, with what he could grasp.

'No, really. I am. Here, let me show you; I'll make fire.'

Richard held his palm out. He called the power from the calm center. Try as he might, nothing happened. He could not make so much as a spark. He sighed as Gratch howled in a roar of laughter, his wings flapping with the joke.

A sudden memory came to him – something Denna had told him. He had asked her how he had done all those things with magic. She had looked at him with that all-knowing smile of peace, and said, *Be proud you made the right choices, Richard, the choices that allowed to happen what came about, but do not call arrogance to your heart by believing that all that happened was your doing.*

Richard wondered where the line was. He realized he had a lot to learn before he was a real wizard. He wasn't even sure he wanted to be a wizard, but he now accepted who he was – one born with the gift, born to be the pebble in the pond, son of Darken Rahl, but lucky enough to have been raised by people who loved him. He felt the hilt of the sword at his elbow. It had been made for him.

He was the Seeker. The true Seeker.

Richard's thoughts again touched the spirit who had brought him more happiness than in life had brought him pain. He was deeply gratified that Denna had found peace. He could want nothing more for her, for someone he loved.

He came out of his thoughts and patted the gar's arm. 'You wait here a minute, Gratch. I'll get you something.'

Richard ran into the kitchen and retrieved a leg of mutton. As he ran back down the steps, Gratch danced from one foot to the other in excitement. Together, they sat on the steps, Richard eating his soup, and Gratch tearing into the meat with his fangs.

When they had finished – Gratch had even eaten the bone – Richard pulled out a long lock of Kahlan's hair.

'This is from the woman I love.' Gratch considered, then looked up as he gently reached out. 'I want you to have it. I told her about you, and what you mean to me. She will love you just as I love you, Gratch. She will never chase you away. You can be with us whenever you want, for as long as you want. Here, give it back a moment.'

Gratch held out the length of hair. Richard took off the thong holding Scarlet's tooth. It would do him no good any longer; he had already called her with it. He tied the long lock of hair to the thong, and then hung the whole thing over Gratch's head.

With a claw, Gratch stroked the long hair. His grin wrinkled his nose and showed the full length of his fangs.

'I'm going to go to her now. Would you like to come along?'

Gratch nodded his enthusiasm, his head bobbing, his ears twitching, and his wings fluttering.

Richard looked down on the city. Troops were moving about. A lot of troops. Imperial Order troops. It wouldn't be long before they gained the courage to investigate the death of the council, even if it was at the hands of a wizard.

Richard smiled. 'Then I guess I better find a horse, and we can be on our way. I think it best if we were away from here.'

He looked out on the brightening day. A breeze with a hint of warmth ruffled his mriswith cape. Before long it would be spring.

to pay him. With the War coming they would need him again. He was the specialist of specialists, totally discreet and terrifyingly effective. He also made a very bad enemy.

'Now?' he asked.

'As soon as you can. If you wait too long, someone might notice. Also we don't want the risk. The Effect is still not perfectly understood. You might not get a second chance.'

The Remover stood. Then he smiled. 'I have never yet needed such a thing.'

He was gone from the inner room so quickly he might have been a shadow flitting across the dark walls. The master of the House of Hellebore could see much that others could not, but even he had trouble marking the exact progress of the Remover's self-deletion.

It would not be good to have to guard against that one, he thought to himself. He must be kept sweet, or he must become ashes in the Well of Forgetting. Either way, he must never again work for one of the other houses. The master of the house stroked the pale flower on his desk again, considering.

Another curiosity of the hellebore is that its bloom can be frozen solid in the deepest winter snows, but when the ice melts away, dripping from the petals like tears, the flower beneath is still alive, still supple. Hellebore is strong and patient.

The tall, lean figure in the spidersilk suit pressed a button on the side of his desk and spoke into the air. The wind carried his words to all those who needed to hear them, throughout the great city and all across the troubled land, summoning his allies and tributaries to the first council of the War of the Flowers.

FOR THE LATEST NEWS AND THE HOTTEST EXCLUSIVES ON ALL YOUR FAVOURITE SF AND FANTASY STARS, SIGN UP FOR:

ORBIT'S <u>FREE</u> MONTHLY E-ZINE

PACKED WITH

BREAKING NEWS
THE LATEST REVIEWS
EXCLUSIVE INTERVIEWS
STUNNING EXTRACTS
SPECIAL OFFERS
BRILLIANT COMPETITIONS

AND A GALAXY OF NEW AND ESTABLISHED SFF STARS!

TO GET A DELICIOUS SLICE OF SFF IN <u>YOUR</u> INBOX EVERY MONTH, SEND YOUR DETAILS BY EMAIL TO: <u>ORBIT.UK@TIMEWARNERBOOKS.CO.UK</u> OR VISIT:

WWW.ORBITBOOKS.CO.UK
THE HOME OF SFF ONLINE

Infinitive	Preterite	Past Participle
Infinitiv	*Präteritum*	*2. Partizip*
werden (du wirst, er wird; werde!)	wurde, *dichter.*: ward (würde)	geworden; *als Hilfsv.*: worden
werfen (du wirfst, er wirft; wirf!)	warf (würfe)	geworfen
¹wiegen	wog (wöge)	gewogen
¹winden	wand (wände)	gewunden
wissen (ich weiß, du weißt, er weiß)	wußte (wüßte)	gewußt
wollen (ich will, du willst, er will)	wollte	gewollt
wringen	wrang (wränge)	gewrungen
zeihen	zieh	geziehen
ziehen	zog (zöge)	gezogen
zwingen	zwang (zwänge)	gezwungen

Weight / Gewichte

1,000 milligrams (mg.)	= 1 gram (g.)	= 15.43 grains
1 000 Milligramm (mg)	= *1 Gramm (g)*	
1,000 grams	= 1 kilogram (kg.)	= 2.205 pounds
1 000 Gramm	= *1 Kilogramm (kg)*	
1,000 kilograms	= 1 tonne (t.)	= 19.684 hundredweight
1 000 Kilogramm	= *1 Tonne (t)*	
	1 grain (gr.)	= 0.065 g
437½ grains	= 1 ounce (oz.)	= 28.35 g
16 ounces	= 1 pound (lb.)	= 0.454 kg
14 pounds	= 1 stone (st.)	= 6.35 kg
112 pounds	= 1 hundredweight (cwt.)	= 50.8 kg
20 hundredweight	= 1 ton (t.)	= 1,016.05 kg

Length / Längenmaße

10 millimetres (mm.)	= 1 centimetre (cm.)	= 0.394 inch
10 Millimeter (mm)	= *1 Zentimeter (cm)*	
100 centimetres	= 1 metre (m.)	= 39.4 inches /
100 Zentimeter	= *1 Meter (m)*	1.094 yards
1,000 metres	= 1 kilometre (km.)	= 0.6214 mile ≈ ⅝ mile
1 000 Meter	= *1 Kilometer (km)*	
	1 inch (in.)	= 25.4 mm
12 inches	= 1 foot (ft.)	= 30.48 cm
3 feet	= 1 yard (yd.)	= 0.914 m
220 yards	= 1 furlong	= 201.17 m
8 furlongs	= 1 mile (m., mi.)	= 1.609 km
1,760 yards	= 1 mile	= 1.609 km

Vulgar fractions and mixed number / Brüche (gemeine Brüche) und gemischte Zahlen

$\frac{1}{2}$	a/one half	*ein halb*
$\frac{1}{3}$	a/one third	*ein drittel*
$\frac{1}{4}$	a/one quarter	*ein viertel*
$\frac{1}{10}$	a/one tenth	*ein zehntel*
$\frac{2}{3}$	two-thirds	*zwei drittel*
$\frac{5}{8}$	five-eighths	*fünf achtel*
$\frac{1}{100}$	a/one hundredth	*ein hundertstel*
$1\frac{1}{2}$	one and a half	*ein[und]einhalb*
$2\frac{1}{4}$	two and a quarter	*zwei[und]einviertel*
$5\frac{3}{10}$	five and three-tenths	*fünf[und]dreizehntel*

Decimal numbers / Dezimalzahlen

0.1	*0,1*	nought point one	*null Komma eins*
0.015	*0,015*	nought point nought one five	*null Komma null eins fünf*
1.43	*1,43*	one point four three	*eins Komma vier drei*
11.70	*11,70*	eleven point seven o [əʊ]	*elf Komma sieben null*